DIARY OF A DRUNK DRIVER

The Complete and Accurate Tale of a Man Arrested For and Convicted of Driving While Intoxicated

MICHAEL A. PALERMO

Copyright © 2020 by Michael Palermo

All rights reserved.

Published by Red Penguin Books

Bellerose Village, New York

No part of this book may be reproduced in any form or by any electronic or mechanical means, including information storage and retrieval systems, without written permission from the author, except for the use of brief quotations in a book review.

To All the Hardworking, Honest, Caring, Self-Sacrificing Police Officers who risk their lives daily!

Contents

Introduction	vii
1. That Day	1
2. The Ride Home	5
3. The Next Day	13
4. Deciding on a Lawyer	19
5. Court	25
6. Life Without a Car	33
7. Conditional License	39
8. The Wait	43
9. The Hearing	47
10. The Interim	51
11. The End of the Year	55
12. Sentencing	59
13. OASAS	61
14. March 2nd, 2012	65
15. Community Service	69
16. OASAS Part 2	73
17. The Ignition Interlock	77
18. Meanwhile	81
19. Suffolk County	85
20. The Drinking Driver Program	89
21. The Victim Impact Panel	91
22. Moving Right Along	95
23. 2013	99
24. End Game	103
Afterword	109
About the Author	113

Introduction

First of all, let me say that it's not a good idea to drink and drive; I'd been doing it for years and getting away with it. Getting away with it because I'd always been careful, cautious, and never drove when I thought I had too much to drink! I was a college baseball coach for seven years and one time, after I got thrown out of a game, I stopped at an Italian restaurant in Bloomfield, New Jersey, to grab something to eat, have a cocktail, and calm down. Who do you think was sitting next to me at the bar? Clete Boyer, the great former Yankee third baseman of the 1960s and the then-third base coach for the Yankees! I looked over at him, smiled, nodded, and thought to myself "Where the hell do I know this guy from!" Then, being a Yankee fan my whole life, it hit me: "This is Clete Boyer!" So, being the ballsy bastard I am, I said, "You're Clete Boyer," and he said, "That's right."

I said, "I bet not a lot of people in here know that!"

He said, "NOBODY FUCKING KNOWS IT and I'd like to keep it that way!" He gave me a look, and I gave him a look, we both laughed and started bullshitting!

I told him I was the head baseball coach at St. Joseph's College on Long Island and we were in town playing Bloomfield College. I explained that we won the first game of a doubleheader and that I was thrown out of the second game, showered, and stopped at this place! He said it must've been late in the game and I must have been way behind. He was right; we were getting our asses kicked 11-2 and it was the next-to-last inning. Anyway the point of all this is that we kind of bonded, kept drinking, and I think he was enjoying the camaraderie. We were talking about all the old Yankees ... all my idols ... Mickey Mantle and his drinking, etc. ... and then he said something to me that I'll never forget! "Sometimes you're better when you have a few in you!" A few. Not shit-faced, not stupid! Just enough to feel better and relaxed.

If I drive over the Verrazano Narrows Bridge between Brooklyn and Staten Island when I'm completely sober, I'm scared to death; my hands are sweating, my heart starts racing, and I can't wait until I've crossed that son of a bitch. But a vodka and a couple of glasses of red wine with dinner and I glide over that baby as relaxed as I can be—not speeding, just gliding! But the problem is, most people don't have a few. They don't know when to stop. Those are the people who are the reason drunk driving and the consequences of it are out of control. Those people are the reason you are reading this book!

1

That Day

I have a friend who once said to me that, "No good deed goes unpunished." And he's so right! The day started off as innocently as could be. I had it all planned. My daughter Mary asked me to install an air conditioner in her apartment. Only one problem: Her apartment was in Hoboken, New Jersey, and I lived in West Babylon, New York. But the temperature had been fluctuating between 98 and 103 degrees in the shade, and if I have one weakness, it's my daughters, Mary and Gina. Mary asked and I said I'd do it. I decided to go on Monday, July 18. I had it all planned! I would get up early, switch cars, and use Gina's Honda CRV with the hatchback, go pick of up one of the air conditioners I had been storing at my father's house, go to the gym, get in a good workout and get to Hoboken by 1:00 PM. I had it all planned; I even texted my ex-wife, Rose, early in the AM to make sure she was leaving that Honda SUV there for me—EVEN THOUGH I HAD REMINDED HER THE DAY BEFORE! Got to the house, guess what? The Honda's NOT there!!! "GODDAMN IT!"

But should I have been surprised? No way—Rose had been pulling stuff like this for 25 years. The funniest part of it is I don't believe it was intentional! For an extremely intelligent girl, she just doesn't think, and it's not her fault; it's the fabric of neglect in her upbringing.

Anyway, I called her at work: "Where's the Honda?"

"I have it!"

"Didn't I ask you to leave it for me? I'm going to Hoboken."

Pause. "Oh my God! I forgot!"

Gina drove me to get the Honda; we switched cars so Rose had a car to get home from work, and I'm off to the old man's house! Get the A/C and I'm off to the gym! The gym and my workout are like therapy to me. With my bad knees, I have fallen in love with the elliptical machine; I get on that bad boy for 30 minutes, level 10, and I'm in another world sweating my ass off! Five-minute cool down, 20 minutes of weights, 10-minute walk on the treadmill, another 5 minutes of light weights, jump in the pool, jump in the Jacuzzi, back for a quick dip in the pool, and I'm READY TO GO!!!!! Shower, shave, and I'm off to Hoboken!

The LIE, short for the Long Island Expressway, is a road that was designed by someone who had the brain of a gnat: Robert Moses. There's not too much traffic for a Monday in July in 105-degree heat! Not too much traffic until you get to the Midtown Tunnel. I pay the toll and negotiate my way into the Big Apple with the sweat pouring from every crevice of this monumental custodian for a plethora of people! I move through the traffic of the city to get to the Lincoln Tunnel. I drive through this tunnel into Jersey and finally I've hit Hoboken—and I'm already exhausted! There's no parking in Hoboken, so as I'm approaching Mary's apartment, I call her from my cell to let her know I'm close; I've just broken the law by using my cell phone, but what the hell! I pull in front of her place, and my day is brightened by the sight of her! "Hi Dad!" Ah! It was worth the trip!

I double-park and as she's watching the car to make sure I don't get a ticket, bad knees and all, I carry that cooling machine up three flights of stairs. With my trusty Phillips head screwdriver, I install that baby in her window in 20 minutes! I come back downstairs, and she's smiling as I tell her it's finished. She goes up to check it out, comes back down, gives me a hug, tells me I'm the best and says, "I'm taking you to lunch!" OK—I'm in!!! Let's go! She knows this great little Italian restaurant, so we're off!

We drive into the heart of Hoboken, the town Frank Sinatra grew up in, and we find a parking spot right across the street from the restaurant. Things are looking up! I put a few quarters in the meter, we cross the street, and we're in! Nice place! The waiter sits us down, gives us the menu, and asks if we'd like a cocktail. DO I WANT A COCKTAIL OR WHAT!!! Mary orders a Coke with lemon and I order a Ketel One on the rocks with a few olives—my mouth is watering!

Mary and I like the same things, so we usually end up splitting stuff: Caprese, an order of broccoli rabe, and penne with wild mushroom sauce was the pick of the day and, in addition to my Ketel One on the rocks with olives, for me a cold glass of Pinot Grigio! No dessert because it was approaching 3:30 PM and I know if I don't hit the road soon, I'll be buried in traffic! The check comes, Mary pays the bill, and we're out of there. I drive Mary back to her apartment and get a big hug, a kiss, and a thank you! I drop her off and I'm on my way!

2

The Ride Home

Anytime I leave Mary or Gina, I get this little sensation in my heart—a sadness, an emptiness—and it's been that way since they were babies. After I got divorced it became even more prevalent, so I tried to do everything possible to see them every day and be there for them all the time. Now I'm alone in Gina's CRV leaving Hoboken, reflective, daydreaming approaching the Tunnel when, guess what, traffic brings me back to reality! It's 4:00 PM and I'm hot and tired and stopped in the Tunnel. After about 40 minutes of what should have been a seven-minute ride, I see light and I'm in New York City with more traffic. "Which is the best way out of this woods?" So I think, well, the Midtown Tunnel must be packed, so let me try the Williamsburg Bridge. I drive toward the Village; it's about 5:30 PM and I'm hot, dry, and there's more traffic. "Let me stop for a quick beer to quench my thirst!" I find an illegal parking spot by a place called "Off the Wagon," rush in, and have two pints of cold Coors Lite and another Ketel One on the rocks. It's Happy Hour, so 10 bucks on the bar covers everything! I rush back to the car and I'm off to the bridge.

Once I plow through the city and get to the bridge the traffic is not too bad, so I'm thinking with any luck I may be home by 7:30 PM. No way. I get over the bridge, hit the BQE, and it's a parking lot! All right—I'm beaten! So I crawl along with the traffic and I'm starting to get hungry. It's a quarter to 7:00; if it stays like this, I'll be home at 9:00 PM and I won't eat 'till 9:30 PM if I'm lucky. In Williamsburg there's Bamonte's, an Italian restaurant that's been there since Christ was a kid. The food is great! I'd been going in there for years. My father grew up in this neighborhood and anytime I was in there for business or whatever reason, I'd stop for a bite to eat. The bartender's name is Mike but everyone calls him Diesel because he's built like a diesel engine. In this neighborhood, everyone had a nickname!

I park the car, walk in the door, and the big guy greets me. "Hey kid, how you doin'? Want a martini?" Well, sure I do, but first I want another Coors Lite; I'm thirsty! Gulp that baby down, the martini is on its way, and I order a grilled chicken Caesar salad with Italian bread. Sip the martini, and just before the food arrives, I'm down to the olives—down the hatch! "Want a wine?" Diesel asks. Sure I do—another Pinot Grigio! Finish my dinner, drink my wine, and naturally the big guy backs me up; before I can open my mouth, a second Pinot Grigio is right in front of me! Now I'm relaxed and feeling nice and refreshed. Holy shit, it's almost 8:30 PM! "Want an espresso, kid?" If I have an espresso, that means a Sambuca and I'm gonna sit here til 9:00 PM! "No thanks, Diesel. Check, please!"

"OK, kid!" I get the check, and considering everything, the big guy takes care of me! I pay cash and tell him "Keep the change, Boss!" "OK, kid. Drive carefully!" I walk to the car and I'm off! Drive through the neighborhood, hit the BQE, over the Kosciuszko Bridge, and on to the LIE. I am exhausted! Traffic is slow but moving steadily. I should be home by 9:30 PM! No baseball games tonight—it's Monday and both the Yankees and Mets are off. I'm stuck listening to WFAN and the assholes who call in; and being exhausted, I'm not in the mood. I'm not in my car so I don't have my CD rack and I wind up shutting off the damn radio.

Traffic is still about the same but I'm bored and tired; nothing on the radio, so what do I do? Like an asshole I start texting and playing with the cell phone! Approaching the Cross Island Parkway—I'm getting closer!!! The Cross Island is clear; I'm moving. I might make it by 9:20 PM! Ah, the Southern State is in view! I hit the exit, glide around the circular curve, and I'm on it! Traffic once again is slow, but moving!

Playing with that phone was a big mistake; because somewhere along the Southern State, I must have changed lanes without signaling! I'm moving along, doing about 40 mph, which is keeping with the flow of traffic. I pass the old tollbooth in Valley Stream; this area where the old tollbooth used to exist is a monumental landmark. When I was a kid, and probably until I was 19 years old, the cost of this toll was a dime; and that dime meant I was on my way to Grandpa and Grandma's house in Brooklyn! I could do another book on my relatives, but I don't want to stray from the theme of this one. I will tell you that my Grandfather, Phil Adamo, was, in my eyes, the epitome of what every man should be: not pretentious, not arrogant, and not crass, but rather strong, funny, loving, caring, intelligent, unassuming, and human! Not perfect, but human! I always looked forward to being with him. I loved him!

Anyway, I'm past the toll area and now I'm past Valley Stream State Park. Shit, if all goes well, I'll be home in 25 minutes. I'm past the Meadowbrook Parkway. On my way!

And then it happened! Blaring siren, lights flashing! I'm in the middle lane so, like I always do when I hear sirens, I pull over to the right so whoever it is can pass and get through. Only this time, the car ain't passing; it's getting behind me! Oh, shit—it's a fucking cop! "PULL OFF THE PARKWAY AND ONTO

THE SHOULDER," he bellows through his loudspeaker. What shoulder? There's only a grass embankment here, so I drive onto it. "STAY IN YOUR CAR!" roars the miked-up voice! The cop strolls over to me. It's a New York State Trooper! He walks up to the window: "License and registration." I nervously take out my wallet. I find the license right in the front; I also have two Police Benevolent Association cards that I can't find among all my other cards. Stupid me—I should have kept them right with the license but, in hindsight, I don't think it would have made a difference with this guy! So I reach in the glove compartment and get the registration. I hand it to him and I know I'm in trouble.

"Have you been drinking tonight?" Oh, shit! Now what the hell am I supposed to do? I know the smell of alcohol is probably permeating through my dehydrated body. I know I'm fucking exhausted and probably look like I'm in bad shape. And I know that lying to this guy ain't gonna help me one bit.

"Yes sir, I had a couple of drinks with dinner."

"STEP OUT OF YOUR CAR!"

Just about that time another trooper pulls up. I step out of my car! The next trooper gets out of his car! The first trooper tells me to walk to the back of my car. I walk back there. Trooper one tells me to stand on one leg. The problem is, I can't stand on one leg when I'm sober! I have no cartilage in both of my knees, no ligaments in my left knee, and only a posterior cruciate ligament in my right knee! I start to laugh and calmly explain this. Trooper two smiles slightly and actually looks like a human being. "I told you stand on one leg; left leg first."

So I do it and naturally I wobble. "Stand on your right leg!"

Again I wobble! He takes out a flashlight and shines the fucking thing right in my eyes. "Look to the left . . . look to the right . . . all right, you're under arrest."

"Oh, come on, fellas, I'll be all right. My friend is a highway patrol cop; I've got two PBA cards. Gimme a br—" Just then the cocksucker hits me with a forearm smash over my left eye. He tries to grab my right arm and pull it behind me so he can cuff me.

I hear "TAKE IT EASY!" from trooper number two. My instincts take over! I wrestled in high school and college and wrestled in the Amateur Athletic Union. I have a brown belt in kenpo, a brown belt in taekwondo, studied budo jiu-jitsu for a year, and boxed for three years. I can handle myself. But I was never a bully or one who looked for trouble; in fact, I always tried to avoid trouble. But this son of a bitch pisses me off, so as he grabs my right arm, I overhook him with my left arm, flip him over, and we both fall to the ground. Trooper two pitches in and between them they manage to get the cuffs on me. I'm bruised on my left elbow and scraped on my left knee, and trooper one has a gash on his left leg!

Trooper two helps me up and looks at trooper one and says "Jesus, he's got cards, his buddy is ... !" Trooper one yells, "I DON'T CARE WHO HE KNOWS!" Trooper two helps me into his car: "You come with me." While we're driving, he explains that he is going to take me back to the trooper barracks in Valley Stream for a while, fill out some paperwork, and then he'll release me!

So I get in his car; the cuffs are tight. I can't believe this has happened! We get to the barracks and trooper two leads me inside, loosens the cuffs, tells me to sit down on a bench, and then proceeds to cuff my right wrist to the arm of the bench.

"What happens next?" I ask. He tells me he's going to fill out some paperwork and I should just sit still, be quiet, and relax. About 10 minutes later trooper one comes in bleeding from his leg. Two paramedics and someone from Internal Affairs come in; one paramedic goes over to trooper one; the other paramedic and the guy from Internal Affairs come over to me, uncuff me, and lead me into another room.

"Are you OK? Do you want to go to the hospital?" HOSPITAL? "For what? I'm fine. I just want to get the hell out of here!" The paramedic looks me over, takes my blood pressure, and they both ask me a few questions. They tell me that when there's an incident like this, Internal Affairs gets involved. The guy from Internal Affairs asks me for a statement as to what happened. I basically tell him what I've told you. I had a few drinks with dinner at Bamonte's, took the BQE to the expressway to the Cross Island to the Parkway, and here I am! I never mention Hoboken or the drinks in the city. They lead me back and I'm cuffed to the bench again.

Both troopers are working at separate computers; trooper one won't even look at me but I notice a big fucking bandage on his leg. Trooper two tells me, "Boy, you're clean as a whistle!" He looks up from his computer, looks me right in the eye, and shakes his head! It's now about 11:00 PM. "Would you please let me call my friend?" I plead. Trooper two tells me to sit tight; both troopers leave the room. About 15 minutes later trooper two comes back and says "All right, who's your friend?" I ask him to please let me have my cell phone back and I'll call him. He gives me the phone and I go to my contact list, look for Zsolt, and press send . . . please answer . . . "Yes, Mikey!!!" I hear. There is a God!

"Zsolt, I'm in trouble!" I explain to him what's happened. He asks to speak to trooper two. Trooper two takes my phone and goes into another room. After about 5 minutes he returns and hands me the phone. Zsolt tells me he's coming to get me, but I have to do whatever they tell me and I have to blow! This means I have to take a breathalyzer! If I don't, I'll automatically lose my license for a year! ALL RIGHT, ALL RIGHT, JUST GET ME THE FUCK OUT OF HERE!

I thank him and put the phone down! Two other troopers come in and lead me to another room; one sits by the door, the other leads me over to a machine. He hands me a slim funnel-like apparatus and tells me to take a deep breath and blow into it and that if I don't blow hard enough, it won't register. I blow as hard as I can! "IS THAT HARD ENOUGH?" He nods his head and smirks! They lead me back to the bench and trooper two tells me to sit down and wait. NO MORE CUFFS! It's now about 11:45 PM and Zsolt shows up. He comes in smiling, introduces himself to the boys, shakes my hand, and asks me if I'm OK. I nod. Trooper two comes over and hands me four computer printouts: summonses! He gives me back my wallet, my phone, and the small amount of cash I had with me. I shake his hand; trooper one is nowhere to be seen. I walk outside with Zsolt to his SUV and we get in. "You OK?" he asks me again. "Yeah, I'm OK; I'm just fucking exhausted!"

Zsolt is the salt of the earth. He's a guy who came to this country as a boy from Romania and is a self-made man. I met him about 15 years ago at Bethpage Auto Repair, a place I had been bringing my cars to for quite a while. He was working there for his uncle and eventually took over the shop. He enlisted in the Marines, became a Nassau County police officer, and was now a well-respected Nassau County Highway Patrolman! I had done him several favors, gave him good advice financially, and brought his repair shop much business. We're friends!

He tells me, "You blew an 0.18!"

"What does that mean?" He proceeds to explain that it means I was more than two times over the legal limit of .08! This is NOT good!

He says I'll need a lawyer. He says there was nothing he could do because it was basically after the fact and that everything was already in the computer. All right; I'll make some calls tomorrow and get myself out of this.

He drops me off where my brand-new Lincoln MKZ is, at my house in Bethpage where my ex-wife and daughter Gina are sound asleep. I thank him again and again! He assures me he was glad to help and that he'd call me tomorrow with the name of a lawyer friend who handles these cases every day. I wait for him to pull away. Then I get in the Lincoln, drive to West Babylon, pull into my apartment complex, take my clothes off, sit on the edge of my bed, and shake my head. WHAT THE FUCK JUST HAPPENED? I lie down and pass out!

3

The Next Day

Did you ever have a terrible dream? A dream so vivid and close to reality that you could swear it happened? I've had 'em and then I'd wake up, shake my head, and not believe it didn't happen. Well, the next morning I woke up, opened my eyes, and I laid in bed staring at the ceiling for about five or six minutes. My mind began to process what HAD happened. I tried to evaluate the enormity of the situation and then it hit me! I GOT A FUCKING DWI! What does this mean, what do I do, who do I call? Oh shit!

I'm a pretty calm individual and I've always been the one not to panic in a time of crisis but, I must admit, I was shaken. "OK, get yourself together, get your ass out of bed and deal with this. You got yourself into it and you'll get yourself out of it. Take a shower, get some coffee, start your day, and do what you have to do!"

I got up, made the bed, went into the bathroom, and began my daily routine: brush my teeth and the three S's—shower, shave, and show me the way out of this! Finished, I look out the window and my Lincoln is still there! I remember that I've got to get Gina's car; dammit, this means I'm pretty sure I'm going to have to tell my ex-wife about this because Gina's car is in her name! I can hear it NOW! This is perfect for her! She's been calling me a "functional alcoholic" for years. Maybe she's right . . . but there's no way I want to let her know about this! All right, let's get some coffee and I'll feel better!

I get in the car and drive to the Dunkin' Donuts right up the block. The girl who's there every morning greets me and I act as if nothing has happened. I get my coffee, sit at a table, and read the newspapers: no box scores from last night. The Yankees and the Mets were both off—remember? So I kind of browse through the *New York Post* and *Newsday*, actually browsing and staring into space at the same time, absolutely not concentrating on anything but the thought of what happened last night! I finish the papers and ask for a refill; I'm going to need one!

Back in the car, back to my place. SHIT! All right—get yourself together! So I go on the Internet and Google DWI in New York State. Oh man—lawyers advertising like you wouldn't believe! Finally, I find a website that tells me what I didn't want to know: I'm in BIG TROUBLE! Not only do I have a DWI, but a 0.18 is an AGGRAVATED DWI—which AIN'T good!!! I read and reread hoping to find some form of a silver lining. No chance! All right, let me call the trooper barracks; maybe if I get trooper two on the phone, I can talk my way out of this!

Recorded message, no voicemail! They ain't talking to no one! All right—I've got to get Gina's car. So I call the impound shop and they tell me what I already knew I didn't want to hear: they'll release the car only to the registered owner, Rosemarie (Rose) Palermo, my ex-wife! Dammit!

Reflecting, I realize how lucky I was. The fact that I was driving Gina's car and not my own allowed me to keep my car. Had it been my car I'm not so sure I would have gotten it back right away! Also, the fact that I was picked up by state troopers and not the Nassau County Police meant that I went to the trooper barracks and not to a holding cell at the County Court in Hempstead to await arraignment in the morning. I also got to hold onto my license for 20 days until my court appearance on August 3rd. But then again, maybe a Nassau County cop would've called Zsolt and I'd have gotten away with it! Who the hell knows?

My mind was racing! I had to get Gina's car and that means I've got to call Rose! She works for a lawyer and is a very intelligent girl! I'm the one who pushed and prodded her to use her skills, get a job, and move her life forward. Now she's in charge of the office and excelling in every aspect of her position.

"Hi, it's me," I sheepishly state. "I know who it is!" she replies matter-of-factly.

"I need you!" I tell her. She asks why and I tell her that I really didn't want to get into it over the phone. I explain that we have to get Gina's car and it could take about an hour.

"Can you meet me when you go to lunch?" Our one common bond is that we both love our children so I knew as soon as I said it was for Gina, we'd be good to go. We agree to meet at the house at 1:00 PM.

Now comes the hard part: I've got to explain the entire scenario to her! She arrives; we get in my car and as we're driving I tell her that I got a DWI last night. Surprisingly calm, she asks, "And you're admitting this to me?"

I laugh, thinking to myself, "I HAVE NO FUCKING CHOICE!"

We get to the impound shop and pick up the car without issue. When we get back to the house, I ask her not to tell the girls, especially Mary; because Mary would probably blame herself! "I'll tell them myself," which I had every intention of doing. Maybe this will be a lesson for everyone!

Between the time I got off the phone with Rose and our 1:00 PM meeting, it became apparent that I was going to need a lawyer. Zsolt told me this when he picked me up. He knew someone who was a criminal lawyer and specialized in DWI cases. I called Zsolt and after he asked me how I was doing, he gave me the phone number. Then I called my buddy Scott Brenker, also a lawyer. Scott is a personal injury attorney; he didn't handle DWI cases but he made a few calls for me and relayed what I already knew: NOT GOOD!

My mind is working: who do I know? Ah, Fred Annibale, my fraternity brother from college. His brother, Bob, and I were pretty tight and I knew Fred specialized in criminal law; I left a message on his voicemail. Called the guy Zsolt recommended, and he suggested I come to his office that afternoon for a conference; bring the citations with you!

OK, one more call: Lee Kleinhardt, a lawyer who got me out of some minor traffic bullshit a few years earlier—seat belt, stop sign, etc. I left Lee a message on his voicemail. Then I called back the guy Zsolt recommended to schedule a conference THAT afternoon. Why wait? Let's see what he's got to say! He schedules me for 2:00 PM reminding me to bring the citations. He tells me the office is in Farmingdale, "Across the street from The Raven's Nest, you know, the strip club you used to go to," he chuckles. I chuckle back, "I was never in there—not my thing!" And it's not my thing! In the 61 years of my life, I think I've been to a strip club four or maybe five times; never understood the infatuation with watching a girl get naked so I might get aroused and walk out of the club with my dick in my hands! We both laugh again. I hang up and get the feeling that this should be an interesting meeting.

I arrive at 2:00 PM. The receptionist asks me to fill out some forms and while doing so a voice booms through a speaker in the lobby! "You want some coffee?" The receptionist laughs,

"That's Keith. Would you like some coffee?" No thanks! She then leads me into a conference room where Keith Lavallee, attorney at law, is sitting at one end of a long conference table with a yellow legal pad in front of him. He stands up, shakes my hand, and invites me to sit down. I hand him the citations and go through the entire story.

Keith seems like a nice guy but is very impressed with himself. I get mixed vibes. He lets me know that state troopers are a problem and informs me that he is aware of who the two of them are. Munoz, trooper one, "has always been a pain in the ass! Let's hope he fucks up between now and when we go to trial —if we have to go to trial!" As far as trooper two, "Soloman is OK—not a bad guy!" He called trooper two, Duchase, by his first name to let me know he knows him on a first-name basis! We go through the conference and he lets me know that he does NOT go to court with me on August 3rd; his associate, Joe Carbone, does. Also, because I'm a friend of Zsolt, his fee is $4,000, and that if he has to attend a conference before a trial or we have to go to trial, there would be an additional fee!

He walks me outside the building and just about that time Joe Carbone drives up and gets out of his car. Joe Carbone is A BIG GUY! Keith introduces us, we shake hands, make some small talk, I thank him and get in my car and drive away.

I'm ambivalent about the situation. The fact that Keith wasn't going to court and that Joe Carbone was just didn't do it for me. The $4,000? Well, let me see what Fred and Kleinhardt have to say! I drive to Nicky's of Centerport to grab something to eat. I'd hung out in there for years, ever since I moved to Huntington after my separation from Rose. I'm hungry and thirsty! Centerport is about 15 miles from Farmingdale and while driving, I'm trying to process all of this. My mind is wandering, and then it occurred to me: it's my sister Jenise's birthday!

4

Deciding on a Lawyer

My sister Jenise was born July 19, 1954, so she was 57 today. I picked up my cell phone and called her! I figured that while I was driving to Centerport, it would keep my mind in another direction!

"Hello Michael!"

"Hello, little sister—happy birthday!" There was a little chill in the conversation because my sister is omnipotent, and over the previous few months we'd been having a disagreement about the care of my parents. Also, she went behind my back and procured power of attorney for my parents' estate WITHOUT MY KNOWLEDGE! It's a long story and, once again, the kind of material that would itself make for an interesting book. We spoke for a while; and I related my memories of when she was born, made her laugh, and we hung up cordially. I never mentioned the prior evening to her. I wasn't in the mood and certainly didn't want to open up the possibility of a potential lecture!

I arrived at Nicky's and, I must admit, I usually would have a Stoli on the rocks with a couple of olives prior to lunch and 2 or

3 glasses of Chardonnay with lunch! Susan, the bartender, was shocked when I ordered a club soda. I am intelligent enough to know that I didn't need to get myself into any more trouble. I had lunch, bullshitted with some of the boys at the bar, and I was off.

I got home about 5:00 PM, checked my messages, and poured myself a vodka. As I'm staring into space for about 15 minutes, the cell phone rings—the caller ID says "restricted"—I answer. "Michael? Lee Kleinhardt. What can I do for you?" I explain everything to him. He listens and tells me that he'd been in court all day taking care of the same issues and says he'll take the case for $2,000, that there's no rush to come into his office because we have until August 3rd, I should get a good night's sleep and not to worry! I explain that I'd contacted a couple of other lawyers and wasn't sure what I was going to do. He says to call him in a few days and let him know what I'd decided! I thank him, tell him I will, and hang up.

At that moment, for some reason, I felt a lot better. "I'm going to use this guy," I thought; but I hadn't heard from Fred Annibale. I'll wait and concentrate on the good things: I've still got my license, I'm alive, no one got hurt, and Kleinhardt made me feel better!

Two days later Fred Annibale still hasn't gotten back to me. I decide to call Kleinhardt, set up an appointment, and go to his office. Never met him before and, as is often the case, he looks nothing like I'd pictured! We sit down, he looks at the tickets and says that he'll take care of me for the two grand he quoted me; knows the judge, and DWIs are not like they used to be. The Nassau County DA is on a mission and that two or three years ago, because I have a pristine record, I'd probably get away with a slap on the wrist.

Kleinhardt puts me in his book and tells me to bring the $1,000 retainer to court that day. The only thing he asks is if I'm not going to use him to let him know in advance. He even tells me where I should park at the courthouse; he says that when he dies he wants to come back as the Chinese guy who owns the parking lot! No pressure; very matter of fact—I like this guy! He also introduces me to his father, Charlie Kleinhardt, who's been a criminal attorney for over 40 years.

I ask Charlie, "I'm in trouble, aren't I?"

"A bit," he says. "But don't worry about it—my son is the best!" Once again I feel better!

Three days later Fred Annibale calls me; I explain what happened. He tells me to come into his office the next Tuesday at 5:00 PM and he'll take care of me! Tuesday rolls around and, coincidentally enough, it's my mother's 85th birthday. I love my mother, so I decide that after I see Fred, I'll drop in on Mom. That day I had appointments set up. I still had to keep working so I could pay for all of this, plus I didn't know how long I'd be without a license; and, maybe most important, working kept my mind off things! About ten minutes to five I pull into the parking lot of the building where Fred had his office. "Head-In Parking Only," the sign said. Not realizing what this meant I had to drive into a spot and since there is no car in front of me I pull forward so that when I get done I won't have to back out—I can just pull away! I walk into the building, find Fred's office, knock on the door, and after a few seconds Fred answers with a warm greeting. I've always liked Fred and always loved and respected his brother, Bob! Bob was like a big brother to me!

I went to Nassau Community College my first two years and, like most 17-year-olds, I wasn't sure what I was getting myself into; and in my case, I was probably more insecure than I led people to believe. I was asked to pledge a fraternity almost immediately but decided against it for several reasons. I was in a high school fraternity, got my ass paddled, had to put up with all the hazing and didn't feel like going through the bullshit again.

Plus, I thought I was in love, I was working part-time at Sears, and planned on going out for the wrestling team, so I didn't need the crap that goes along with pledging a fraternity. But those guys kept after me, especially Bob, and we became good friends. So in the second semester I relented; in retrospect it was an experience. I met some nice people, met some babes, etc. Hell night was a blast—myself and the three other guys I pledged with got basically tarred and feathered, blindfolded, and dropped off somewhere with supposedly NO money. Bobby found a way to slip me $50 bucks! It was the night Martin Luther King Jr. was assassinated in 1968. We were dropped off in Shirley, New York, which is way out on eastern Long Island; we didn't know where the fuck we were. Bobby's $50 came in handy!

Fred leads me back to his office as we make small talk. He tells me to sit down as I hand him the summonses. He looks them over and I could see his mind working, trying to find something wrong or some loophole. Right up front, I tell him I've seen Lavallee and Kleinhardt. Fred tells me Lee's a good lawyer and asks if Lavallee introduced me to Joe Carbone. Yes, I tell him, and he informs me that Keith lets Carbone handle these things until there's a trial. Fred's up front with me; as I've found out, they're not fooling around with DWIs in Nassau County. Fred tells me he'll be with me all the time, gives me info about Judge Goodsell who handles these things, tells me I'll have to go for OASAS counseling and I'll have to put an interlock device in my car! He tells me the interlock is "a pain in the ass!" Boy was he right—but we'll get to that later!

Fred assures me, as did Kleinhardt, that he'd keep me out of jail —for five grand! He tells me not to worry and to use the lawyer I feel comfortable with, and that no matter what I chose to do I could call him anytime, once again indicating that Kleinhardt is a good lawyer. When I look back I kind of think he didn't want to be involved and I never saw him in court, but I did call him on a few occasions and he returned my calls. We shook hands, and I left the office, walked to my car, and what do you think I found? A FUCKING PARKING TICKET! Head-in parking means you can't pull forward; the ASS of your car has to be showing. This was a sign; five grand and a parking ticket? I called Kleinhardt the next day!

While driving away from Fred's office I was actually laughing!

Now, I'm going to see Mom. My sister Jenise and her family are there having dinner. I kiss Mommy, give her the little stuffed animal I bought her, and, after they invited me to join them, I left! I wanted to get some take out, go home, take my suit off, put my shorts on, have a cocktail, eat with a glass of wine, relax, and go to bed! Besides, as I mentioned earlier, there was a coolness between us having to do with the caretaker we were using. I felt my sister usurped her position, plus I wasn't too fond of my father. I loved him, always did, but there was always, for some reason, an inherent disregard.

I finally got to bed, up the next day, and went through the rest of the week working with pretty much a business-as-usual attitude—except I wasn't drinking and driving. No more late-afternoon lunches with a few cocktails. I was just biding my time!

Saturday rolled around. I got up, went to the gym for a light workout, and decided to go to the beach. I love the beach; it's always relaxed me. Back at home, the phone rings: "Hi, Mr. Palermo, this is Christine, Gina's friend. Gina's OK, but we're at the hospital!"

"Well, if you're at the hospital, then she's not OK!" She tells me what hospital, and like a shot I'm dressed, in the car, and ON MY WAY!

I get there, walk into the emergency room, and there's Gina with a shit-eating grin on her face. Christine had explained to me on the phone that they had gotten drunk the night before and that as they were lying in the sun, Gina began to feel dizzy and lightheaded.

When I saw her face I knew she was OK! "Hi Daddy!" and we both started to laugh. She told me what happened; the doctor had already examined her and determined that there were more serious cases in the emergency room but would call her to come in for a final look see. I asked her if she called her mother. "Yes, Daddy." She calls me "Daddy" with a little whimper in her voice when she knows she's getting away with something. She tells me Mommy didn't answer and she didn't want to scare her by leaving a message. OK. I decide to get her home and tell her mother then.

Now I couldn't very well reprimand my daughter after I'd just gotten a DWI, so we talked about it—and maybe we both learned a lesson! The nurse brought us in to see the doc; he took her pulse, said everything was normal. He laughingly told her to stay off the booze! We got her home and her mother was there! "Please come in with me, Daddy!" OK, who do you think got the lecture? Not Gina. "She's my daughter, she's in the hospital, and you don't call me?" I'll leave the rest to your imagination!

5

Court

Wednesday, August 3rd, finally rolls around! I get up early and for some reason I'm not really nervous— maybe a little apprehensive, but not nervous. I slept good the night before so I was relatively relaxed. I put on my blue blazer, light blue trousers, and a white shirt with a red and blue silk tie. I look good! I'm off; drive to a Dunkin Donuts, have a coffee and a muffin, read the paper, and hit the Southern State Parkway about 8:15 AM. The court is in the town of Hempstead, which is about two steps above Tijuana, Cleveland, and Buffalo when it comes to the dirtiest places I've ever been to! I graduated from Hofstra University, also located in Hempstead, in 1972 so I'm very familiar with the area. Hofstra is actually located in a nice section of town; it borders East Meadow, Merrick, and Uniondale. But downtown Hempstead is pretty much a pit!

I find the parking lot right across the street from the court and, just like Kleinhardt said, there's a very pleasant Chinese guy there, smiling, as he takes your money! As I walk to the court, I notice the police vans with the cages that transport the criminals to jail! Hmmm, I think to myself, wonder if I'm gonna be in one of those? No, Lee promised me I wasn't going to jail! I get to the courthouse door, wait on the line, and finally get up to the walk-through barrier. The cop tells me to take everything out of my pockets, place them in the basket, and walk through! No problem. I get in, put the stuff back in my pockets, and find the rotunda in the middle of the courthouse where Kleinhardt told me to meet him. While I'm waiting, I notice the calendars posted on the wall. I look for my name ... There it is on the criminal calendar—TWICE! What? The troopers had also charged me with RESISTING ARREST!

Lee arrives, and I show him the calendars. He says I didn't tell him about the resisting arrest! What happened was that there was another summons attached to the DWI summons and, not realizing it, *I had inadvertently taken notes on it* like it was a piece of scrap paper. I HAD NEVER SHOWN IT TO ANY OF THE ATTORNEYS!

Lee asks me how much money I have on me; I said just the grand you asked me to bring.

"We have time; you better find an ATM and get yourself another grand!"

Oh, shit! So I walk out of the courthouse and hurry to the parking lot, which is now full. I explain my dilemma to the smiling Chinese man. "You leave, you pay again!" YOU PAY AGAIN in that fucking Chinese accent! OK, you cocksucker. I ask him if there is a TD Bank nearby. He's not sure, so I start walking. I ask a gentleman approaching me: "Hey buddy, is there a TD Bank around here?" He tells me there's one about 5 or 6 blocks away and points me in the direction. I'm now sweating; it's August and about 90 degrees.

I start walking swiftly. I find the bank, but you can only take $700 out of the ATM, so I've got to wait on line! Thank the Lord the line is not too long; I get the thousand bucks and start walking, almost in a slight jog, back to the courthouse. Through security, inside, and I'm really sweating. I see Lee.

"Did you get it?" YES, I got it! He tells me to relax, go in the bathroom and wash my face because we have a few minutes. We take the stairs up to the courtroom on the third floor. We take the stairs because Lee doesn't trust the elevators! When we get inside the courtroom, Lee tells me he knows this judge! Judge Votsolonis, who he says he'd helped out when she was having a problem with another case.

"Michael Palermo." They call my name. The assistant DA starts reading all this shit out and starts actually making shit up about my hitting another car. The judge tells him I don't see any of that here in the complaint as she looks at Lee! How do you plead to the DWI and the resisting arrest? Not guilty! OK, so no bail; you're free to go but you have to surrender your license!

In New York State, anytime you are charged with a DWI you automatically lose your license for 30 days and you can get a conditional license until your trial. You can also ask for a hardship license during that 30-day period. I tell Lee I need the hardship license in order to continue to work. He tells me we'll come back on Monday; he has another case then, so he'll be in court. We'll go before Judge David Goodsell; he's the judge who will handle my case until it's over. Lee says Judge Votsolonis always liked him and his father; and because of that and the fact that I was dressed nicely and had an impeccable prior record, she made my life easy. Now I had to take this paper they gave me to the clerk and get it stamped. I had a temporary license until 5:00 PM!

I got the temporary and walked out of the courthouse into the parking lot; it's now about 11:30 AM. I see the Chinese man. He smiles: 25 dollars please! Hey, I've got over a thousand bucks in my pocket—what's 25? I give it to him, get in my car, and drive off. Oh shit! What a morning!

I drive to my mother's house, stop by for 15 minutes, kiss her goodbye, and leave. She doesn't look good but she's pretty coherent. I'm glad I went; don't know when I'll be able to get there again with no fucking license!

I'm hot and sweaty! I drive back to West Babylon. I'm going to the beach—I've got until 5:00 PM! I change my clothes, get to the beach, dive into the water, take a swim, come out, lay in my chair, start reading the paper, and pass out! I sleep for about 35 minutes, wake up, take another swim, lay out to dry, and I'm on my way! I get back to my place and take a quick shower. I'd better do some shopping; 5:00 PM is fast approaching! I get back home, have a vodka, cook myself some fish with veggies, and wait for the ballgames to start. Mets and Yanks on TV tonight!

Today is Saturday! I get up, quick shower, walk to the nearby DD, coffee, muffin, read the papers, and walk back home! Get on the computer, read my emails, etc. Shit, the rent is due! With everything going on, I let the rent slip by. No problem—I've got until the tenth before I get a late charge and they start breaking my balls. I'll just write out a check, put it in an envelope, and go to the post office. Wait . . . I have no license! All right, calm down. The post office isn't that far; I can walk! So I take the envelope and I begin to walk. It's a beautiful day, about 9:30 AM, not really that hot, and I'm actually enjoying the walk! Get there and mail the rent. The post office was about a mile and a quarter from my place and, as I'm walking back, I start laughing to myself: "You better get used to this!"

I get home, take out my guitar, and start playing. The guitar always relaxes me and is a good way to pass the time. I'll delve into my musical career a little bit later on because it winds up playing a role, actually a major role, in all of this. I'd like to go to the beach, so I call my daughter Gina to see if she'd like to go. I tell her I'll make lunch and we'll go to the ocean, Robert

Moses State Park. She's in! Now I've got to get food for lunch . . . walking again! ShopRite is across the street. I pick up some turkey breast, Swiss, tomatoes, chips, a couple of cans of 7Up, walk back, make lunch, put it in the cooler, and Gina arrives! "Hi, Daddy!" Big hug, big kiss!

We take my Lincoln; she drives, of course! Great day—the water and waves are beautiful. We eat lunch, lie in the sun, read the papers, and stay until about 3:00 PM. She drives back; I kiss her goodbye, "Thank you, Daddy . . . I had fun!" Thank you! I take a shower and walk to a little Japanese restaurant around the corner. I've done more walking today than I have in years! Order sake, BIG sake, miso soup, and chicken teriyaki; I sit at the sushi bar with a TV right in front of me. The 4 o'clock Yankees game is on! More sake . . . walk back, catch the end of the game, and a 7 o'clock Mets game is on . . . and I fall asleep in my chair. Get up, go to bed, and I wake up to Sunday morning!

I walk to the bagel store on the corner next to the DD; the owner, Eddie, is a real nice guy. We always hit it off: "You walked over!"

"Yeah! Nice morning!" I order two eggs, bacon, American cheese in a wrap with coffee. As I'm reading the Sunday papers, it hits me: I gotta go to court tomorrow but I've got no license. Oh, shit! I decide to call Dr. Claps, a pal of mine since 1984 when I first moved back from Los Angeles. He's a great chiropractor, but that's another long story! I think I'll give a little insight into this one! When I was a boy, I always had pain in my lower back; I played sports with it, but never could bend over and touch my toes! I don't remember when or how I developed this, but I do know it was there for as long as I could remember. I started lifting weights when I was about 13, but I wasn't allowed to keep the weights in my room where it was warm because my parents were afraid I'd ruin the floor, so they were in the unfinished basement where it was cold and damp. I think I aggravated my back there. I never warmed up properly and never cooled down properly, so instead of ruining that floor, I ruined my back.

When I started working at Sears during my freshman year in college, one of the managers in the automotive section, Stu, took a liking to me; in fact, all of the guys who worked there liked me! These were guys in their fifties and to me, a 17-year-old, they were the salt of the earth. One day when I was in the store basement moving cases of motor oil, Stu noticed that I bent over awkwardly. "Why do you bend that way?" I explained the situation. It turned out that Stu had almost died several years earlier and had his life saved by a chiropractor. Stu was now a health food fanatic, constantly eating sunflower seeds with raisins, etc. He got me an appointment with his chiropractor, Dr. Dale. After three treatments I could touch my toes for the first time in my life. I became a believer and have been using chiropractors ever since. One day, after I moved back to New York from LA, I called Dr. Dale for an adjustment. Dr. Claps answered the phone! He had bought the practice from Dr. Dale. Dr. Claps and I became lifelong friends. We have everything in common from sports to booze to politics!

So I called him, told him the story, and asked if he could pick me up on Monday morning. Not a problem! I didn't really want to inconvenience him too much, so I asked him to drive me to the house on Ginny Lane where I would ask my ex-wife, Rosemarie, to drive me to the courthouse. Why would I do such a foolish thing? The answer is I'm fucking crazy. They say the definition of crazy is repeating the same mistake over and over and expecting a different result! Anyway, I explained the situation to her and she was very accommodating. I love her but, for whatever reasons, after a time we couldn't live together anymore. So Dr. Claps picks me up right on time at 7:30 AM, drives me to Ginny Lane, and Rosemarie is ready to go. We stop for coffee and arrive at the courthouse about 8:20 AM. "Good luck!" she says. I almost wanted to kiss her goodbye! But I thought better of it and didn't!

I'm early, so I decide to walk around and see if I can find a coffee shop. For the first time it hits me like a ton of bricks: I'll never drink and drive again! Walking through and around Hempstead is enough to wake anyone up! I don't know why, with all the bullshit I went through on Friday and before, but it hit me now! Fuck the coffee—I walk back to the courthouse, through security, and wait for Lee. He arrives about 9:35 AM and, like Friday, we walk upstairs to the courtroom. This time I have to wait, and I see a lot of shit! I see lawyers convicted of DWIs, I see blacks, whites, Asians, and children of all ages! I see two guys get turned down for hardship licenses and then, just before lunch, I see Judge Goodsell turn down a hardship license for a guy who's wife has a brain tumor and he needs to get back and forth from New Jersey so he can spend as much time with her as he could! Now, I don't know how true his story was; but it was lunchtime, 12:00, and my case was next, after lunch, about 2:00 or 2:30 PM.

I said to Lee, "I just saw the judge turn down this poor bastard. What fucking chance do I have?" Lee was done for the day and wanted to get out of there, too! I asked him if he could give me a ride to the train station by his office in Baldwin; he dropped me off and I took the next train from Baldwin to Babylon.

I arrived in Babylon about 2:00 PM and immediately went to the Argyle, a relatively upscale restaurant in town. I sat at the bar, ordered a Stoli on the rocks with olives, and began to contemplate. It was Monday, August 8, 2011; I could get my restricted license on September 6, the day after Labor Day, so I had to go a month without a license. It was the summer, and everything I needed was relatively close, even the town of Babylon where there were restaurants and bars. If I needed to go somewhere not within walking distance, there were taxis and the bus. I ordered another Stoli and the menu. I had lunch with a couple of glasses of wine, made small talk with the people sitting at the bar, and began to feel much better! I had money in the bank, my health, my sanity, good friends, and wonderful daughters.

All of a sudden it was after 4:00 PM! I paid the bill and walked outside to find it was raining! Fuck it, I'll call a cab! So I walk into a little trinket shop a couple of doors down and ask the proprietor if he knows where I can get a cab. Amazingly, he has the number. I pull out my cell phone and he says, "That's OK. I'll call for you; the phone is right here!" In 10 minutes the cab shows up, I get home in 5 minutes—7 bucks. Thank you! I'm home! I walk upstairs, change into my shorts, sit in my chair, put the TV on, and pass out!

6

Life Without a Car

The next day I began life without a car! I got up, took my daily morning shower, walked to the Dunkin Donuts, ordered coffee and a muffin, read the paper, and walked back. Beautiful day! Went to the computer, checked my bank accounts, checked the mail, did some paperwork, and pretty much began the day in a somewhat routine fashion. I realized that I needed a workout. How am I going to get to the gym? Let me call my cousin, Louis!

Louis is like my brother. We grew up together. His mother and my mom are sisters. He was my best man and I was his best man. He's godfather to my daughter and I'm godfather to his son. "Looooie, how are you!" I proceeded to tell him I needed a favor; I needed a ride to the Hilton, the gym. Without hesitation he says OK, what time? No questions asked! My response is whatever time is good for you. So he picks me up about 12:15 PM; I've got a bag packed and he's right on time. I'm downstairs waiting for him.

"Where's your car?" "Right over there!" I tell him, pointing to the parking lot! He looks at me and, smiling, asks me what happened. I tell him the truth. "I got a DWI!" We both laugh a little as I tell him the story. Louis is the best! No expectations, no lectures, no bullshit. We'd been through too much together since we were kids. He tells me anytime I need a ride to just call him. I knew that already!

He drops me off and I go to the locker room and it's just like a normal day: I change my clothes, go into the gym, and begin my workout! Elliptical 35 minutes, 20 minutes of weights, 10 minutes on the treadmill, 5 more minutes of weights, pool, Jacuzzi, pool again, shower, shave, back into my street clothes and I'm ready to leave! I feel great! Hmmm . . . How the hell am I going to get home?

The mind starts working! The Hilton has a shuttle from the hotel that will take you in any direction for about 5 or 6 miles. One of the drivers, Al, also works out in the gym; and, when our schedules coincide, we bullshit as we both work out. Nice guy! So I wonder if he's driving the shuttle today. I ask at the front desk and yes, he is; he's on a run but should be back shortly. So I sit in the lobby and wait patiently. Sure enough, about 10 minutes later he pulls up! "Hey Al, I was wondering if you could do me a favor?" I ask. "What do you need, kid?" I tell him that I need a ride into the town of Bethpage, which is just about 5 miles from the hotel. No problem! I get in the shuttle bus and he drives me into town. And there it is: B.K. Sweeney's Bar and Grille! Vodka, lunch, and wine! I'm all set!

After finishing my lunch and half way through my second glass of wine, it occurred to me that I had to find a way home! My place in West Babylon was about 10 miles from Sweeney's. It was a beautiful summer day and about a little after 4:00 PM, so being outside was not a problem. I was a little tired from working out and the day in general. I knew eventually that I was going to have to get used to taking the bus, so I decided now was as good a time as ever. I paid the bill, picked up my duffle bag, and began walking to the nearest bus stop about three blocks away. Got there and waited; sure enough, about 10 minutes later the N81 bus arrived. The N stands for Nassau County; the only problem was that I was going to Suffolk County. I knew this, but I figured once I got on any bus the driver would steer me in the right direction.

I was right. I got on and paid the fair, one dollar, and started to ask questions. The driver, a nice African American man, stopped me in my tracks: "Just tell me where you're going!" I told him and he informed me that this bus would take me up to Hempstead Turnpike where I could catch the N72, which goes to the Babylon train station. Then he hands me this little slip of paper. "What's this?" A transfer. No new fare, so I was getting a ride all the way to Babylon for a BUCK! OK, I'm in! I sit down, it was air-conditioned, and we arrive at Hempstead Turnpike. I walk across the street where the driver told me to wait for the next bus; 5 minutes later it arrives, I get on, hand the driver the transfer, and I'm on my way! I hadn't been on public transportation in years and, I must admit, it's an interesting experience; you meet people who are the salt of the earth on the bus!

The N72 proceeds down Hempstead Turnpike and follows it until it forks to the right on Route 109 in Farmingdale. As we were riding, I strike up a conversation with a black guy who's got a Yankee hat on. "Yankee fan?" I ask. "Been one for 60 years!" He then proceeds to tell me that he was born in South Carolina, moved to the Lower East Side of New York City when he was 10, and moved to Wyandanch about 45 years ago; he's a real nice guy! I take a guess that he's between 70 and 75 years old. "I'll be 73 in November!" he proudly tells me. He looks great! Anyway we start talking sports: the Yankees, the Knicks, etc., and all of a sudden I realize that the bus is approaching a stop on Route 109 right by the ShopRite across the street from where I live! Amazing—this wasn't so bad! I tell him I've got to get off here, shake his hand, get up, and I'm home!

After that day I started taking the bus as often as I could! The next morning I got up and walked to the bagel shop, came back home, got on the computer, and googled Suffolk and Nassau County buses. I was impressed; I could take a bus to the town of Babylon, I could take a bus to the Hilton when I wanted to go to the gym; and, if I mapped it out correctly, I could take the bus almost anywhere I needed to go! So I adjusted! Most of all was that fact that I could take the bus to and from the town of Babylon! Babylon had restaurants, bars, and a smoke shop where I could pick up cigars and actually sit down, smoke a cigar, and bullshit with the other guys who did the same: doctors, lawyers, architects, etc., all kinds of guys who, instead of going into a bar, would stop in the smoke shop, buy a cigar, sit in a big chair, smoke it, and solve the problems of the world!

So for the next 30 days about three or four days a week I would trek into Babylon. If it was a nice day I'd walk; it's about a mile and a half walk so I'd get my exercise in! Either way, the S25 was the bus that I could pick up or be let off across the street from my place. The driver was a nice black woman who told me she'd been driving for over 20 years and was going to retire in December! After a few rides she'd actually let me off right in front of my place! So I slipped her 10 bucks one afternoon and never had to pay again!

The bus ride was always interesting, mostly minorities. I always felt like they'd be looking at me, wondering what the hell I was doing riding the bus! Anyway, I'd get to Babylon usually about 2:00 or 2:30 in the afternoon, have a couple of Stolis on the rocks, order lunch, have a couple of glasses of wine, stop in the smoke shop, smoke, and then make my way home!

At the beginning I'd go into the Argyle; but I found a class of people there that weren't exactly my cup of tea, including the bartender who I called "Ponytail Paul." He was a nice enough guy but a little too impressed with himself for me! Plus, I never trusted guys who were bald and grew the back of their hair long and put it in a ponytail; I never trusted people who wore toupees, either! So I started looking for another place to have lunch and found Lily Flanagan's, an Irish pub right as you first got into town. I'd always known Lily's was there, but I'd never tried it. One day I figured I'd give it a shot, and I loved the place! The bartender, Dwayne, was a hell of a nice guy; and we hit it off right a way! He was from Ireland and was a rugby player and a real down-to-earth guy! I had played rugby at Hofstra; they had a club team and needed players! One of my wrestling buddies was in the club and challenged me to come to the field one afternoon. I had no idea what rugby was; but when he told me I didn't have the balls to play it, I became curious! So I joined the club and I learned to love the game. I only played that one Fall; but I'll tell you, in my opinion, if the game was promoted properly here in the States, it could become very popular. I've often wondered why these rugby players who wear no equipment, hit just as hard, scrum just as rough, tackle just as violently as the players in the National Football League who wear equipment that compares to a suit of armor, never get hurt yet the NFL players suffer all kinds of injuries! Maybe it's the equipment!

So for the month of August, on the days I didn't go to the gym either by bus or by getting a ride from Louis, these were my days! Wake up, shower, and shave, go for coffee, read the papers, do some work on the computer, play the guitar, go into town either by bus or walking, have a few drinks, lunch, have a smoke, return home, watch baseball, go to sleep, get up and do it again. I was under a wonderful house arrest!

7

Conditional License

The month of August seemed to fly by! All of a sudden it was September and the end of my license suspension—the end of life without wheels!

September 2nd was a Friday and we were having a hurricane! My parents' caretaker was worried and, to be perfectly honest, scared! It had rained hard all of Friday night and the winds were very strong, shaking the trees violently and causing the lights to flicker on and off. So I agreed to spend Saturday night at my parents' house. I called Dr. Claps early Saturday morning, and he agreed to pick me up in Babylon and drive me to my parents' house. Great friend! My sister was happy and thanked me several times. I cooked a nice meal for all, had a few glasses of wine with my father, and spent the night sleeping in the basement on a futon. Not a good thing if you want to keep your back together! I woke up Sunday, had breakfast, and the sun was shining!

I called Mary and asked her if she could take me back to Babylon. She agreed and spent the afternoon with me. We went down to the pier at Bergen Point on the Great South Bay. Mary liked to go there and feed the seagulls with me. When we got there, the pier was destroyed from the hurricane—completely demolished! We couldn't believe the damage.

I was eligible to get my conditional license on Monday, September 5th; however, that was Labor Day and all government offices were closed. I asked Mary if she could pick me up early on Tuesday and take me to the Department of Motor Vehicles so I could get my license. Naturally, she said she would. Mary is a teacher and the school semester didn't start until that Wednesday. I spent Labor Day just hanging out—the usual stuff, DD in the morning, walked to ShopRite, had a few cocktails, watched baseball, made dinner, and went to sleep!

The next morning Mary was at my place right on time 7:45 AM. The DMV opened at 8:30 AM and I wanted to get their as early as possible! Going to the DMV is a pain in the ass! The lines are long and the smells that permeate the building sometimes leave you on the verge of nausea! Got there at 8:15 AM and already the line was forming around the building! I told Mary that I wasn't sure how long I'd be and I would text her when I was done. What a child! She had to get up, drive from Bethpage to Babylon to pick me up, drive back to the DMV in Bethpage, pick me up and drive me back to Babylon, then drive herself home to Bethpage! Finally, the doors to the DMV open and the line is not as bad as I thought!

I went through the usual procedures: wait on the first line, tell the woman why you're there, get a form and a number, and wait for your number to be called! After about a half hour I'm called; I explain my situation to an extremely nice woman who couldn't have been more helpful! On the license, you are allowed to pick three locations that become designated destinations you are able to go to and from without a problem. She tells me to go over to a desk, take my time, fill out the form, and walk back up to her when I'm done.

Hmm! My brain tells me to pick three locations that are miles apart from each other at different sections of Long Island. I pick an Insurance office in Valley Stream where the people love me, my buddy's insurance office in Melville right next to the Hilton where the gym is, and a mortgage office in Syosset! So, basically from my place in Babylon wherever I am, I'm on my way to or from one of these places. I go back to the nice lady and give her the form. She smiles, I pay the fee, and I've got my conditional license! Mary picks me up, drives me back to Babylon, and I offer to buy her lunch at Spanakopita! That means Greek food! I tell her I'll meet her back at Ginny Lane in about an hour. I get in the house, go on the computer, do some work, and get ready to leave! Walk to my 2011 Lincoln, start that baby up, and I'm on my way! I've got wheels again!

The Wait

September is basically the beginning of the year for everyone as they wind down from the summer: back to school, back to work, back from vacation, and, for me, back to having wheels even if it was with a conditional license! Each day I scheduled an appointment within the parameters of the restrictive locations on the license.

September came and went. I had a call from my attorney, Lee, reminding me that my next appearance in court was set for Thursday, November 3rd. I wanted to postpone it if possible, but Lee suggested I go there and see what the DA was offering in lieu of a trial.

October was also uneventful except Mary's birthday was on Monday, the 3rd. She was off that day and I believe she had taken a personal day. I spent most of the day working, and in my travels I was able to negotiate a trip to Macy's at the South Shore Mall in Bay Shore. I picked her up a few gifts and got back to my place around 3:30 PM. I had invited Mary for dinner and had made a reservation for 5:30 PM at a nice little Italian place in Babylon. She was to come by about 5:00 PM, so I had a little time to catch up on some loose ends from the day. One of the loose ends was to finish a song I had started writing about three years prior.

The song was originally a theme song for Mike Francesca, a sports disc jockey on WFAN radio in New York City. At the time he had broken up with his partner, Chris Russo, and was looking for a new theme song. I wrote one, went into the studio, recorded it, and sent it over to Marc Chernoff, the manager of the station. They rejected it! Fast forward to 2011. In 2008 the team of Boomer Esiason and Craig Carton had taken over the morning show on WFAN after Don Imus was fired! Imus was the victim of reverse discrimination! He had made an off-the-cuff funny, flippant, totally innocent remark about the woman's basketball team of Rutgers University! Believe me when I tell you in all my years of listening to this guy and other shock jocks, what he said was like a pimple on a camel's ass! But the groundswell of opinion had taken its toll, and Imus was forced off the air! At the beginning I couldn't listen to Boomer and Carton—in fact, I thought they were terrible! ESPN Radio had a morning show called "Mike and Mike" that was equally terrible, if not worse; but they were simulcast on ESPN TV so I watched it. In 2010, I believe, Boomer and Carton's show began to be simulcast on the MSG Network in New York. What piqued my interest was that I wanted to see what Craig Carton looked like. So one morning instead of "Mike and Mike," I flipped the channel to "Boomer and Carton." I liked it! The more I watched, the more it grew on me—they had come a long way, especially Boomer! They were pretty fucking funny; I couldn't turn it off! So every morning at 6:00 AM while lying in bed just waking up, the show was on. It was on in the bedroom and in the living room!

One day I decided they needed a theme song. So I rewrote the lyrics to the Francesca track and today, on Mary's birthday, I was putting the finishing touches on it. I eventually went back in the studio and rerecorded it! At the end of October I sent it over to the producer of the show, Al Dukes, and as I'm waking up two days later, they're playing the thing to open the show! They liked it! Son of a bitch! Al Dukes called me that afternoon and told me they liked it!

Back to dinner with Mary. She arrives right on time! I give her a big "Happy Birthday" kiss and hug, hand over the gifts, and we're on our way to Babylon. We have a great dinner, some laughs, do a little walking through the town, and we're on our way back to my place. Mary has work the next so morning so she drops me off with a big hug, kiss, and "I love you, Daddy!" As she's driving away I get that same feeling in my stomach—you know the one I get whenever I leave my children!

Except for the "Boomer and Carton" song thing, October is pretty uneventful. I continue to negotiate my way around Long Island with my conditional license and I wait for November 3rd. One thing is for sure, I'm not drinking and driving!

9

The Hearing

The hearing date was set for Thursday, November 3rd. On Friday, October 28th, my cell phone rang about 7:00 PM. The caller ID said restricted so I knew it had to be lawyer Lee. "Michael . . . lawyer Kleinhardt . . . how are you?" He went on to explain that he had gotten the report back from the DA's office and wanted to go over it with me; could I come to his office tomorrow morning? So we made an appointment for about 11:00 AM. I got up early. It was Saturday so, as I usually do, I packed a duffle bag and went straight to the gym. Got in a good workout, showered, and mini-shaved—a small shave, just the sides of the face and under the neck—I leave the goatee!

When I got to Lee's office he was finishing up with another client, a young kid, second DWI and, obviously, other troubles! "Come on in!" Lee pulls out the DA report and tells me it's not good! It says that the troopers got a 911 call earlier that evening about a motorist swerving on the Northern State Parkway heading on to the Meadowbrook Parkway; I never even took the Northern State! From the beginning I was consistent that I had taken the LIE to the Cross Island Parkway.

Then he showed me the picture they took of me at the troopers' barracks the night they arrested me. I looked terrible: exhausted and fucked up, with a shit-eating grin on my face! He proceeded to explain that the resisting arrest charge wasn't going to help! He said he'd take it to trial if I wanted him to. It would cost me about $10,000, which he'd be happy to take from me; but he didn't think it was a good idea. At that moment I decided I wanted to see if he could postpone the hearing until after the holidays. He told me to show up on the 3rd and he'd do what he could!

November 3rd arrives and I go to court. Park in the Chinese guy's parking lot, get to court, and wait for Lee. He arrives as usual about 9:35; we walk upstairs and proceed into the courtroom. Lee asks for a postponement. About 10 minutes later the bailiff calls him to the front—they're not postponing anything. Lee tells me he'll talk to the assistant DA and see what he can plea bargain for! About 20 minutes later he comes back to me and says, "You just hit the jackpot, man!" What the hell does that mean? He proceeds to explain that the troopers will drop the resisting arrest and bring it down to a disorderly conduct! He tells me to plead guilty to the DWI and I'll get off with a jail walk-through, three years probation, 50 hours of community service, and an interlock device in my car for as long as I'm on probation—plus a fine! Wonder-fucking-ful! I have 15 minutes to think about it before Judge Goodsell wants an answer! Holy shit!

I tell Lee, "I'm pleading not guilty—fuck 'em! Damn it!!!" Lee looks me in the eye!

"Are you out of your mind? Michael, you're an intelligent man!" He talks me into it; tells me three years probation is usually cut in half and says if I plead not guilty, it goes to trial! Then, if I'm found guilty, it's at least a year in jail not to mention the 10 grand and having to do all of the shit anyway!

Goodsell reads the charges. Lee tells him guilty; Goodsell asks if in the last 48 hours I did drugs, consumed alcohol, etc. He asks if I'm making this decision on my own: "Has anyone influenced you in any way? Has anyone promised you anything in return for your plea?" He sets sentencing for Friday, January 6, 2012!

After leaving the courthouse I had to report to the probation office in Mineola to register for what would become the beginning of my three years probation after sentencing. I drive over, go through security, hand them the slip I was given at the courthouse, fill out the paperwork, and wait. My name is called, they take me in the back, take a DNA sample by swabbing the saliva from my mouth, and tell me a probation officer will be in touch with me. There was one thing that I neglected, and it was important! Lee told me I had to go through OASAS counseling in the meantime. Fred Annibale, Keith Lavallee, and Lee all told me from the beginning that I would have to go through OASAS evaluation and counseling for people arrested for DWI! I didn't understand the evaluation part, nor did I understand that this evaluation was mandatory for sentencing; all I heard was the counseling part. Counseling? Shit, I don't need no counseling! I get it! Don't drink and drive! What the hell do I need counseling for? So I ignored it. When I left court, I was just glad to get the hell out of there!

10

The Interim

The following Tuesday was Election Day. Judge Goodsell was running for another term. I didn't vote for him! Got up, did the usual stuff; while watching "Boomer and Carton," for some strange reason, I decided to send Al Dukes, the producer of the show, an email. "Would love to come in and do the 'Boomer and Carton' jingle live anytime!"

I left my place to vote. I was still registered in Levittown so I decided to stop by and see my parents. I told the old man I was going to vote and he said he wanted to go with me. So I took him! When we got there, he was confused!

I had to kind of walk him through it—he seemed happy, though, and I was glad I took him! I dropped him off and stopped at the library so I could go on line and check my emails before my drive back to Babylon! I went to the address I had emailed Al Dukes from: "How about tomorrow morning at 9:00 AM?"

What? They want me to come to the studio tomorrow to perform this "Boomer and Carton" jingle? So I email him back. "Sure, but I can't put the whole band together . . . it'll just be me and an acoustic guitar!" He emails me back that it's OK, asks me for credentials, tells me to show up about 8:30 AM, go to the guard at the main desk, and there will be a pass waiting for me. All right, I'm in!

I get back to Babylon and I must have practiced the tune 20 times before I went to bed. Next morning I wake up at 6:00 AM to do the show. I slept well and, for some strange reason, I wasn't nervous at all! I decided to dress up: full shave, light blue slacks, printed blue shirt, and my dark blue blazer! Stopped at DD and only had coffee; without eating anything. The juices from the caffeine would be flowing! Read the paper, got a full refill of coffee, and I'm on my way!

The day was a beautiful, sunny, crisp November day. November 9th, coincidentally enough, would have been my twenty-sixth wedding anniversary! Very little traffic. I took the Southern State to the Belt Parkway and through the Brooklyn Battery Tunnel to 345 Hudson Street where the WFAN and CBS studios were located. I found a parking lot about a block away, grabbed my guitar from the back seat, and here we go!

I decided the night before to take my acoustic EKO guitar. I bought the EKO in a hock shop in Huntington about 10 years earlier when my wife and I first separated. I felt comfortable with it! I tell the security guard who I am. He asks for identification, so I show him my driver's license, which naturally has the name Michael Palermo on it. I told Al Dukes in my email that Erik Kyle was my stage name! I get the pass, walk through security, and I'm in. Go up to the fifth floor to the studio. I ask for Al and they point me to the studio where the show was on the air! Everyone made me feel extremely comfortable. Al, Eddie Scozare, the engineer, everyone!

I told Al that he was taking a real shot having me on live having never heard me before! Eddie explained: "Al is so disgusted by all this Paterno bullshit that he was ready to start picking people off the street!" We all laughed and they both assured me they were kidding! This occurred during the middle of the Joe Paterno-Penn State sex scandal. Everyone was jumping on that bandwagon; it had become a national nightmare! Al asked me how I felt and I assured him he'd be happy! All of a sudden I'M ON! The video is on YouTube! It couldn't have gone better; everyone was thrilled, nothing but compliments! I hung around until the end of the show, we took pictures, and I was out of there! As I walked back to the car, even though it was only about 10:30 in the morning, I wanted a drink! NO Way ... I've got to drive back to Babylon! Prior to my DWI, I would've got to the car, put the guitar in the trunk and, since any parking over an hour was an all-day fee anyway, I would've found a bar, found another one with a lunch menu, and made a day of it. Nope—I'm gonna enjoy what just happened on the show, thank God, and drive back home!

11

The End of the Year

The rest of November was pretty uneventful. I received many compliments about my appearance on the B&C Show! Al Dukes emailed the next day and thanked me, telling me how much everyone enjoyed it. We took pictures after the show that became available online through the CBS website! Let me reiterate that everyone on that show treated me wonderfully. I was able to procure a video of the show from the people at MSG that is viewable on YouTube!

The Monday before Thanksgiving, about 9:30 in the morning, my cell phone rang. I didn't recognize the number so I let it go to voicemail. It was my first probation officer! Officer Shannon wanted me to call her back when I got the message. So I did—immediately! We set up an appointment for the following Monday morning after the Thanksgiving weekend. It was for an evaluation and explanation of probation.

Thanksgiving arrived and I made the mistake of spending it at my parents' house with my sister's family! She decided to take her family to the parade in the city; I got stuck cooking the turkey. We were supposed to eat at 4:00 PM—naturally, she didn't show up until 5:30 PM; and, because her lateness threw my father's schedule off, dad got sick. The caretaker was upset and, as usual, was constantly complaining about my sister—never to her face, mind you—always behind her back!

My sister's family left about a quarter to eight, and I was going to leave soon after. Mary was going to pick me up and drive me back to Babylon; I'd had a few drinks and I knew I would be at least drinking wine so I had made prior arrangements. About 15 or 20 minutes after my sister left, my father became very pale; he went into the bathroom and began vomiting! I followed him in and he told me he was dizzy. So I walked him to his room, helped him change, and got him into bed.

I decided to spend the night! I called Mary, told her Grandpa was not feeling well and she didn't have to worry about coming to get me. Neli, the caretaker, seemed happy I was staying. I decided to sleep upstairs in the spare bedroom with the big king-sized bed rather than ruin my back on the futon in the basement. The spare room upstairs is across the hall from Neli's room; I explained to Neli about the futon and the fact that we would be on the same floor didn't seem to bother her! I slept like a baby!

My father slept all night without incident. The next morning he was up bright and early and didn't remember a fucking thing: didn't remember Thanksgiving, didn't remember my sister being there, and didn't remember puking his guts out!

About one week later I get a message from Jenise's husband, Nick. He tells me that Neli was upset about my sleeping upstairs —I couldn't believe it! So the next day I went over to my father's house and approached Neli about it. She said that it didn't bother her at all! So I called my sister. I leave her a voicemail on her cell phone. That night I get a text from Nick and we start going back and forth—he tells me my father wasn't that sick—I tell him he was! Next I get a text from Jenise; we start going back and forth and when I explain how uncomfortable the futon was on my back, she tells me I SHOULD HAVE SLEPT ON THE FLOOR! I couldn't believe it! This was the beginning of a complete schism in our relationship!

As Christmas approached, plans for us getting together became muddled; and, to be perfectly frank, I really didn't want to be around her! However, because my girls enjoyed seeing their cousins, I was willing to suck it up. Then a strange thing happened. For 25 years, even when I was married, Christmas Eve was spent with my family. That was what my mother had always wanted! We would either have it at my mother's house, my house, or Jenise's house. My sister Donna, because she lived in Massachusetts, usually came down to spend it with us. Then Christmas Day was spent with the opposite family. After my wife and I separated, we agreed that Christmas Eve would be spent with my family and Christmas Day would be spent with her family. It worked out well. This year, all of a sudden, the plans changed. It became the opposite, and I wasn't that unhappy!

So I spent a quiet Christmas Eve with my two daughters. They came over, we exchanged gifts, we watched the Giants beat the Jets on their way to their second improbable Super Bowl victory, went to church, and I took them out to dinner. They seemed to enjoy it. The town of Babylon was decorated, the church service was beautiful, and the Italian food was great! We got done about 10:30 PM; they drove so I could enjoy a few cocktails and it turned out to be a quiet, peaceful evening.

The girls spent Christmas Day with their Mom, I saw my parents in the morning and spent a very enjoyable day at my cousin Danielle's house with Louis and the rest of my cousins! My cousin, Danielle, is the best. A beautiful person both inside and out! For some reason we always had a special bond; and I think if there is such thing as a previous life, we had a relationship!

A few days later, just before New Years Eve, I saw Mary. She seemed upset, cold, and kind of distant. At first she told me nothing was wrong but, after my continuous prodding, I finally got her to open up. She told me that Jenise told her I was an alcoholic! I couldn't believe it and it pissed me off that my sister would dare to upset and hurt my daughter by saying something like that about me, something that wasn't true!!! I would never do anything like that to her children, never anything I knew would upset them, even if I thought it was accurate. I would tell her to her face!!! But then, after putting two and two together, what was happening was built upon the seeds of a sibling rivalry. There are many things that are completely irrelevant to this memoir. I will tell you that I always tried to be a loving, caring, protective and supportive Big Brother to both of my sisters. As my wonderful Aunt Eleanore used to say, "There are three sides to every story: side one, side two and the truth!"

New Year's Eve came and went! I spent it alone! Cooked, watched football, had a few drinks, smoked cigars, popped champagne at midnight, and watched the "The Honeymooners" marathon. HAPPY NEW YEAR!

12

Sentencing

Sentencing was set for Friday, January 13th, 2012. It was originally set for January 6th; however, Lee had a conflict so the change was made! I was actually happy for two reasons. One, it gave me another week and two, I had an Alumni Wrestling reunion at Island Trees High School on the night of the 6th! I enjoyed the reunions. Saw my old teammates and got to reminisce about my high school days. Fun night!

Friday the 13th; how's that for a sentencing date? It arrived and I woke up once again not nervous at all. Lee told me what to anticipate. Arrived at the courthouse at 9:30 AM. Same protocol, only this time I took the elevator up to the third floor and waited for Lee. He showed up through the door from the stairwell about 9:45 AM! We walked into the courtroom together, sat down, and waited to be called. About 10:30 AM the clerk called my name, and Judge Goodsell asked Lee to approach the bench. Lee comes walking back to me.

"You didn't go to OASAS . . . I've been telling you to go there for months!"

So what does that mean?

"You're lucky Goodsell is in a good mood or he likes you or something, but he's giving you 6 weeks to go through the OASAS evaluation . . . we have to come back on Friday, March 2nd!" So I walk out of the courthouse basically a free man for six more weeks.

13

OASAS

OASAS stands for Office of Alcohol and Substance Abuse Services. It's a counseling service and evaluation program for people with DWIs, alcoholics, drug addicts, and basically all who have had a run-in of some sort with the law. Lee had given me a list of OASAS centers way back when I first met him. Zsolt's nephew Tommy had told me about a center named PEOPLE in Bethpage. Tommy had a DWI conviction at one time; and when he found out about mine, he recommended that center to me. Tommy told me they were wonderful. Naturally, I ignored him just as I had ignored Lee's instruction to sign up for the program. Because I had ignored Lee, I had disposed of the list he gave me. So I went online and looked up the program. There was a list of centers. The closest one to me was in Amityville. It was called South Oaks and I must have, in my travels, passed it at least a hundred times! I gave them a call.

In order to be admitted, I had to go in for an evaluation. My health insurance plan, Healthy New York, did NOT cover drug and alcohol rehabilitation services, so any cost would come out of my pocket! Of course, there was a fee just to be evaluated. I made an appointment, put on a jacket and tie, and showed up. Introduced myself at the desk and paid the evaluation fee of 100 bucks!

The girl gave me an application and a questionnaire. The questionnaire was a doozy! Questions ranging from "Were you beaten by your parents?" to "What is your goal in life?" I gave it back and sat in the waiting area patiently. The people in the waiting room were, like on the bus, children of all ages. I was the only one in a jacket and tie, and quite frankly, felt that I was way out of my element! Most of the people were in jeans and were minorities! "Michael Palermo!" a voice called out. I looked up and a smiling-faced, a red-headed woman in her early sixties was standing there with my paperwork. Her name was Edna. I followed her into her office and she told me to sit down. I could tell she was looking at me curiously as if she was surprised to see someone like me but, then again, not surprised. The interview began. She read over my questionnaire and asking me in more detail the same questions wanting more specific explanations.

She explained that I'd have to come twice a week for at least six months: once a week for an individual session and once a week for group. She was very nice. I liked her and thought to myself she must have been a beautiful woman in her younger days! I asked her a few questions relating to the program and personnel. I found out she was an equestrian; we seemed to hit it off!

Then she told me I had to take a *breathalyzer* test! OK! I'm clean —I looked at her kind of like, you really think I've been drinking?

Before I could get a word out, she said, "I've had people like you who couldn't face this and actually had a drink or two before they came in here!" So I blew in the tube! ZERO!

She told me she knew that would be the case, but she was just following the rules. I understood. She walked me to the desk, shook my hand and I set up my schedule. The cost: 80 bucks for each private session and 40 bucks for group, 120 bucks a week for six months; and that was the discounted rate! OUCH!

I started my meetings the following week. I'd go to the group meetings on Tuesday night at 7:00 PM and see Edna on Thursday mornings at 10:00 AM. The meetings with Edna were fine and kind of therapeutic in their own way. We'd talk about a range of things; but mostly, she wanted to make sure that I understood the seriousness of the consequences of drinking and driving.

The group meetings were another story. First of all, they were held in a meeting room in the basement of the building. The place was filthy, dingy, with walls of peeling paint and, worst of all, as depressing as they could make it. The people in the group were obviously very troubled individuals. Drug addicts, heroin addicts, alcoholics, spousal abusers, you name it. There was one guy who, like me, was a first-time DWI offender. He was already in his tenth month of probation. Family guy, in his late 40s, married with children. He made good money as an electronics sales rep, something he'd been doing for over 20 years. We kind of gravitated to each other. Nice guy! I would pick his brain about probation and all the things that went along with it.

One night after our meeting, he took me to his car to check out the interlock device. He showed me what he had to do in order to start the car: press a button, wait for a beep, blow into the tube, and wait for another beep that signaled it was OK to turn the ignition key. Man—I wasn't looking forward to this!

The meetings continued for six weeks or right up until March 2nd, the day of sentencing. In the group sessions, we'd see movies of addicts, alcoholics, etc., and we'd have discussions that I really didn't find helpful to me. I knew what the deal was, and I never considered myself an alcoholic, just someone stupid enough to make the mistake I made.

In one group session, a counselor went around the room asking each person if they were ashamed of themselves. Everyone either said yes or was reluctant to say no! When she got to me, I said I was NOT ashamed; I made a mistake, admitted it to myself, admitted it to members of my family, and I was going to do my penance and move on. I think that kind of startled her; she was an old-school counselor. There was also a younger woman counselor who said I should be proud of myself for feeling that way, and the two of them kind of went at it for a few minutes. Bottom line: we all make mistakes! Just try not to make the same mistake twice!

14

March 2nd, 2012

I continued at South Oaks right up until my sentencing date of Friday, March 3rd. I had changed my group session from Tuesday evenings to Tuesday mornings. After the group session on the morning of February 28th, I went into Edna's office and reminded her about my sentencing. She was aware of it and told me she had already prepared a letter that was being sent to the DA's office, the court, and my attorney. We talked for a few minutes and I asked her if it was necessary for me to come in Thursday for the private session. She told me it was not and wished me luck at the sentencing. "What kind of luck?" I thought to myself. I asked her if I could get a copy of the letter; it basically said that I had been evaluated for alcohol abuse and that all my subsequent drug and alcohol tests were negative. March 2nd arrived—again not nervous! I pretty much knew what to expect; a jail walk through, a fine, 50 hours of community service, three years of probation, and the interlock device in my car for the duration of my probation!

Lee prepared me. Did my morning daily—showered, etc. Dressed in a sport coat and slacks with a pullover shirt. No tie! I had coffee at the DD and drove to the courthouse. Parked at the

Chinese lot, walked through security, elevator up to the courtroom, and waited for Lee. When he arrived, we went inside and waited to be called. "Michael Palermo," the clerk called out. As Lee and I walked through the swinging gate, two cops, one male and one female, began to approach and stood behind me!

Judge Goodsell began reading the DWI charge I had pled guilty to. He looked at me kind of like, "I'm just doing my job . . . " He asked me if I had anything to drink or had done any drugs in the last 48 hours, if anyone influenced my decision, if anyone had promised me anything, etc. He then read my sentence and as he did, the female cop grabbed my right hand, then my left hand, pulled them behind my back; and for the second time in my life, I was handcuffed!

After the judge was finished, the cops led me past the judge's bench, through a door and down a staircase to the basement where there was a series of holding cells! Before we approached the holding cells, we stopped; and the male officer told me he had to search me. He asked me if I was OK. I said I was and said: "I screwed up!" He didn't say anything! Then the female officer told me to follow her. He was behind me and I followed her in front of me as they walked me to a cell. We stopped and I apprehensively looked inside. Then she told me to follow her again.

They walked me to a door, removed the handcuffs, opened the door, and told me to report to the officer who was by the door that led to the outside of the building! "You're free, good luck!" said the male officer and gave me a smile! I smiled back and thanked them both. THAT WAS IT! I walked over to the officer by the door, signed something, she gave me a piece of paper, and I left. I now had to go upstairs, pay my fine, and get my probation papers. I began looking for Lee but couldn't find him; so I went to the clerk's office, paid the fine, and got the papers. As I walked out of the office, Lee called my name! "You all right?"

I asked him where he'd been, and he told me he was in the basement looking for me. "That was the quickest jail walk-through in history!" he laughed. We went over the probation papers to make sure I understood them. I was to immediately report to the probation center in Mineola. I left the courthouse, walked to the parking lot, paid the Chinese guy, and made my way to Mineola. When I arrived, as I walked through security, I made eye contact with one of the guards I'd seen the first time I was there. After I went to the desk and checked in, I walked back over to him; and he started bullshitting with me.

He asked me why I was there and when I told him, he said in a very cynical way: "It figures. It's all about the money. A guy like you the cops should take it easy on . . . shoulda let you go . . . sons of bitches! In the old days they woulda drove you home. Nassau cop?" he asked. When I told him it was a trooper he replied, "Oh, those cocksuckers . . . they're real bastards!"

Just then the woman called my name. "That's me." "Good luck, kid!" As I walked back to the office, he had me thinking, "Yeah, those bastards. They should've let me go!"

The girl led me into a room, and there was my probation officer. "Officer Tobias," he says as he shakes my hand, "Sit down, son!" Now he, as well as the guard I just spoke to, are probably my age, yet they're calling me son and kid! Officer Tobias explains to me that since I live in Suffolk County, they're going to eventually move my case. Tells me it will probably take a couple of months. In the meantime, I could get started with him. He tells me I'm clean as a whistle, nothing prior and he's going to be as easy as he can be. He gives me some paperwork and tells me all I have to do is fill out this one sheet and fax it back to him once a month! He's a human being, very nice and certainly not looking to break my balls! He also explains that I have a 20-day stay: 20 days with the temporary license they gave me at the courthouse to get the interlock installed in my car. After the twentieth day, I

CAN'T DRIVE ANY CAR THAT DOESN'T HAVE ONE! He gives me a list of the three interlock companies certified by the state. After I get it installed, I'm to come back with the installation certificate; and he'll give me a letter I'm to take to the DMV to get my interlock-restricted license. He also gives me the telephone number and the address where I have to set up my community service. I have 48 hours to call them and make an appointment.

15

Community Service

There are so many parts and facets to probation that I think it's best to break it down into sections, starting with community service. As soon as Lee informed me back in November that part of my sentencing would be to participate in 50 hours of community service, my mind began to work! I started asking questions. What was it? What did I have to do? I received a wide range of answers from putting on a janitor's uniform while picking up debris along the Southern State Parkway, to washing dishes and cleaning toilets in a nursing home. I thought that maybe I could turn this into a positive experience for everyone.

As I noted earlier, I sing and play the guitar. About a mile from where I lived was Sunrise Village, a senior community home. The Monday after my sentencing, as instructed, I called the community service office where I was to report and made an appointment for Thursday, March 8th. After I hung up the phone, I took a ride over to Sunrise. I parked the car and walked through the front door like I owned the place. I went up to the receptionist and asked who was in charge of activities. "Maryanne McGrath!" I asked to see her and was told her office was upstairs. No appointment, no call, nothing! So I went upstairs and found her. "Maryanne McGrath?" I asked as I stuck out my hand. "Michael Palermo, how are you?" She was adorable, about 28-30, 5'3", chestnut brown hair and an angelic face. She responded by taking my hand cautiously while looking at me inquisitively.

"You probably won't believe this, but I'm a criminal," I told her while she looked at me in disbelief. Smiling, I went on to explain the entire situation: that I'd been convicted of DWI, needed 50 hours of community service, I sang and played the guitar and that I would come there once a week and entertain for free! She looked me with a blank face and still hadn't said a word! All of a sudden she blurted out, "Come with me!" She walked me into another room, opened a desk drawer, and handing me an application said "Fill this out." I filled it out and as I brought it back to her, she began to smile! I explained about my upcoming appointment on Thursday. She gave me her card, "Have them call me!" I couldn't thank her enough as she said, "You're welcome" with a kind of sympathetic look. I went to my appointment on Thursday, filled out another application, met with another pleasant young woman, Mayra Portillo, explained the situation giving her Maryanne's card and, somewhat to my surprise, she was amenable to the entire idea! "I think it's great," she told me.

Sunday afternoon Maryanne called and asked me to come in to make out a schedule. I went to see her on Monday, and we set up a schedule for two hours every Wednesday afternoon from 3-5:00 PM. First, I would do an hour upstairs; and then I would go down to the main floor and do the second hour. The folks upstairs were people who needed some form of long-term care. They were not fully capacitated and had dementia, Alzheimer's, etc. I'd sit on a chair and the aides would put them in a circle around me. Without any sheet music, I'd play everything that existed in my memory bank, from originals to '50s and '60s music. They loved it!

The people downstairs were a little more complicated. They were relatively alert and needed aid but not long-term care. After I finished upstairs, I'd do the second show downstairs. I would set up outside the main lobby just before the dining room. Again, from memory, I'd play basically the same *repertoire*.

One afternoon, I think it was the third week, a crusty old woman who I was told was never happy, snapped at me: "Don't you know any other songs?" I looked at her and, after suppressing a little anger, thought to myself. "This bitch is right!" So I asked her if there was any song in particular she wanted to hear! "Crazy!" She exclaimed! I had always liked the tune written by Patsy Cline—probably the most popular rendition of it was done by Willie Nelson. I told her I'd learn it and do it the following week.

I asked other folks if there were any more requests. I got several, including "How Great Thou Art." That night I went to the computer, found the website chordie.com, and began downloading songs. Every week I'd download two or three new songs and eventually I put together a "fake" book that I still have today. Later on I found out that the woman who requested "How Great Thou Art" was blind; I'd play it for her every week and she couldn't thank me enough! They all seemed to thoroughly enjoy the shows.

As I was building up my hours, Maryanne and I developed what I would like to think became a friendship. One day she asked me if I wanted to come in on Mondays for an hour and call Bingo. So getting into May with three hours a week, I was slowly eating up my community service hours. In June I called Mayra and asked her if she minded if I found another Senior Village so I could burn up more hours. She told me she might know of a place. She called me back about an hour later and gave me the phone number of the Farmingdale Adult Day Care Center. I was to contact Brandi. I called and set up an hour that Friday morning at 11:00 AM.

I got there a little early. The center was located in the basement of a Lutheran Church. For some reason, I was a little nervous. The people at this location only required, or could only afford, day care. In other words, unlike Sunrise, they got there at 8:30 AM and left at 3:00 PM—it was day care! I played until 12:00. When I was done, Brandi said, "You're fucking great; thank you!" She signed my sheet, and I've been going there ever since. Now I do it because it makes me feel good. Brandi was good to me while I was on probation, and it keeps my chops up! By the end of June between Sunrise and Farmingdale, I'd accumulated over 50 hours! I kept performing at Farmingdale and still do.

Sunrise was another story. Politics reared its ugly head there and Maryanne was replaced. About a month earlier she had confided in me that something was going on behind her back. She was upset by it and I felt for her! Coincidentally, the person who fired and eventually replaced her was a friend of my sister Jenise! Maryanne was treated unfairly. Maryanne is probably better off. I never saw her again, but I won't forget her kindness!

16

OASAS Part 2

After sentencing and after setting up community service, I decided that I needed to change the venue for my OASAS counseling. South Oaks was way too expensive and, quite frankly, not a nice place. Edna was wonderful; but the place, the inmates if you will, and the overall environment was something I thought I might be able to improve on. So I decided to try PEOPLE, the place Zsolt's nephew Tommy recommended. I set up an appointment for Monday, March 14th, at 2:00 PM. I had my interview with Shari, another charming young woman with a beautiful face. The interview was very similar to the one at South Oaks. She informed me that there were random urine tests and that if I wanted to be accepted, I would have to take a urine test that day.

I had been drinking over the weekend; not anything crazy, but a few vodkas, wine with my dinners, and anisette with my after-dinner espresso. I told her I would NOT submit to a urine test that day. My probation orders specifically stated that I was to stay completely away from alcohol for the duration. At South Oaks, they were only giving me breathalyzers, so I could drink a little the day before and I would blow zero at my sessions. Shari also told me that any time I had spent at South Oaks would not count toward my service time at PEOPLE. I would have to start over. I told her I wanted to think about the change.

I left for the Bethpage library; I went online and googled "how long does alcohol stay in your system?" The answers were vague, ranging from 24 hours to 3 days. PEOPLE was a lot less expensive than South Oaks; $20 a session, $40 a week as opposed to the $140 per week I'd been paying! I also knew I would be having the interlock installed in my car within a few days and that the device could be very sensitive. So I made an executive decision. I would STOP drinking completely! From that day on until the end of my probation, I didn't have a sip; not even a freakin' penne a la vodka!

I called Shari the next morning and set up my appointment for Thursday afternoon: Monday, Tuesday, Wednesday, Thursday afternoon. "Shit, I should be clean by then; I'm not a fucking alcoholic!" I thought to myself. So I went back Thursday, took my urine test, and set up my first sessions for the following week. They were every Wednesday and Thursday night at 6:00 PM. There were no private sessions at PEOPLE, just two groups, one analytical with discussion and one educational.

The place was great. I actually almost looked forward to the sessions. The counselors were terrific! The leader of the center, Bryant Kaplan, was cool! He ran one of the sessions one night and made a statement about meditation and how he never got upset. Then he kind of got into it with one of the kids in the group and I challenged him and defended the kid; Bryant's face became red as a beet, clearly pissed off! I reminded him that he never got upset. It gave him pause and after the class he came over to me and we had a laugh about it; it was a nice moment.

The guy I liked the most there was Will. Will was a big African American guy who ran the analytic/therapeutic group. He loved discussions. Every week we'd talk about how our individual past week had gone. I had no problem revealing what I had been through; my life basically was the same. I worked, went to the gym, played the guitar, and watched sports. In fact, all of this occurred during LINSANITY, maybe the most exciting era in recent New York Knicks history. LINSANITY was the Jeremy Lin era; the portion of the 2012 basketball season that was such that I couldn't wait to get home and watch the Knicks. I'd always smoked cigars but now, I guess as a substitute, I'd smoke one or two every day, but only at night and only after I ate. So I'd rush out after my session, take out my cell phone and call the pizza restaurant near where I lived, order half a hero sandwich (usually peppers and egg with pepperoni), pick it up, rush home, turn on the TV, change my clothes, watch the game while eating, clean up, make coffee, sit down and relax while I smoked my cigar. I was enjoying myself!

17

The Ignition Interlock

Probably the biggest pain in the proverbial ass throughout probation was the ignition interlock. A couple of days after I left Officer Tobias I called the three interlock companies that were on the list he had given me. I also had done some research prior to my sentencing. Naturally, each company told you why they had the best program. Several factors went into my decision for the company I eventually chose: money, location, research, and the overall feeling from the representative I spoke with over the phone. I chose the Interceptor Ignition Interlock. I had 20 days from my sentencing to get the thing installed, get a letter from Officer Tobias, and go to the DMV to get my new restricted license; the restriction being that I could only drive a car that had the device! So I made my appointment for Thursday, March 22nd—the 20th day! One of the reasons I chose the Interceptor was the company's location. It was way out on Long Island in Shirley. I didn't want to be near anyone and Shirley is about as far out as you can get.

My appointment was for 9:00 AM. They were very nice. The installation fee was almost $200! I signed the contract, gave them a credit card so they could bill the monthly fee of 100 bucks, and drove around the building to the garage where a kid named Brian was waiting for me. I say a kid; he looked like a kid but was actually in his early 30s. Very matter-of-fact guy! It took him about 45 minutes to install the thing. When he was done, he called me over for a demonstration. Put the key in the ignition and turned it to accessories; DO NOT try to start the son of a bitch! If you do it's got to be reset, which takes 4 days and costs 25 bucks each time.

"PLEASE WAIT!" A moderate female voice calls out from the speaker that was installed on the dashboard. About 3 seconds later the voice commands, "PLEASE PROVIDE A SAMPLE!" You then have to take this little black rectangular box and blow into the tubular mouthpiece on the top of it. You blow for about 3 to 4 seconds and it cuts off; then you wait. "YOU MAY START THE VEHICLE, THANK YOU!" You've got a minute to start the vehicle or it resets and you've got to go through this again! If you don't blow hard enough, "INVALID SAMPLE. PLEASE TRY AGAIN." Holy shit.

Brian walks me through this a couple of times. He also explains and points out that there's a freakin' CAMERA that he installed right in the middle of the dashboard so the people at probation know it's you. Can't fool these bastards! All right. It is what it is; but here's the real kicker: While you're driving, at any fucking moment, you might hear, "PLEASE WAIT. PLEASE PROVIDE A SAMPLE!" And you've got to go through the process!

I leave the garage, find my way to the LIE, and, as I'm driving to Mineola to see Officer Tobias, wait for this thing to go off! I kept the radio off; I have to admit I was nervous! The way Brian explained it to me, if you give an invalid sample you have to blow again. If you give another invalid sample, you get one more shot. After that, or if God forbid you've been drinking, ALL HELL breaks loose: sirens, whistles, a voice that tells you to get off the road and shut down the car and the cops are called. Holy shit, was I fucking nervous! After about 15 minutes I heard the voice; "PLEASE WAIT. PLEASE PROVIDE A SAMPLE!" I blew in the box until I heard a click and waited. "ROLLING RETEST PASSED. THANK YOU!" You're welcome! I'm still nervous because I don't know when this thing is going to go off again!

I get to Mineola and about 5 minutes from the probation center, as I was daydreaming, the thing goes off again. Semi-startled, I went through the process, " ROLLING RETEST PASSED. THANK YOU," just as I approached the parking lot. I parked the car, walked across the street, through security, saw Tobias and gave him the certificate Brian gave me, and got the letter I needed to take to the DMV. I went back to the car, went through the process, started the car, had one rolling retest and got to the DMV in Bethpage about 3:00 PM. I stood on line for about 20 minutes, got my license, and was out of there! That night I had an OASAS meeting at PEOPLE. I was starving so I went to a local pizza/Italian restaurant and had the early bird special with a nice Coca-Cola!

After a while I got used to the interlock. The initial start wasn't too bad; the pain in the ass was the rolling retest. I felt it was dangerous, especially at night and in traffic. Obviously, I never had a failure; however, a couple of times, maybe two or three, I had to retest because I hadn't blown hard enough. By law, every two months I'd have to go back to the Interceptor shop and get what they called a recalibration.

One afternoon, after playing at Sunrise, I got in the car, went through the normal routine, and heard, "YOU MAY NOT START THE VEHICLE!" I didn't know what to do. So I tried again and nothing happened. I had Brian's cell phone number in my glove compartment and immediately called him and told him what happened. It was a hot day in May and, without thinking, I had parked in the sun. Apparently, the heat had an affect! Brian told me I'd have to wait about 5 minutes for the device to reset. I did; the car started! Brian informed me that I had 4 days to bring the car back to the shop for a reset.

I made an appointment and while I was there waiting a guy drove up and said hello to me. He got out of his car an introduced himself: "John Ruocco." He extended his hand, I introduced myself and we began to bullshit. It turns out he was the owner of the company. Very nice man! He asked me what I did; and when he found out I was an insurance broker, he began picking my brain! He was looking for a company to give him an exclusive agency for anyone who had a DWI and had the Interceptor installed in their vehicle. I thought about it and decided that there could be a nice commission attached to it, so I shopped it to several companies! This went on for a few months, and every time I'd go for a recalibration we'd chat. No insurance companies were interested but John and I developed a relationship: he was also looking for investors and I got the feeling he was having some problems!

My instincts were correct. He eventually lost his contract with New York State! People like me who already had the Interceptor were grandfathered in and were able to keep it for a while. In my 14th month of probation I had to have it replaced. The State of New York had revoked his contract entirely. I had a feeling there was some political motive involved. I was right. In February 2014, a guy named Gary Melius, the owner of the Oheka Castle, an exclusive catering facility on the North Shore of Long Island, was shot! Melius was an investor in the Interceptor, a political fundraiser, and from what I've gathered through news accounts, had gained control of the company! For several weeks after the shooting, the Long Island newspaper *Newsday* printed detailed investigative reports, including information about the relationship between Ruocco and Melius.

18

Meanwhile

During probation, despite all of the complications it brought, I had a life to live. I continued to work and I decided to get a mortgage loan originator's license. I had been a mortgage loan officer for years. In 2008 after the shit hit the fan with the banking crisis, I pretty much stopped. The Dodd-Frank Act, the SAFE Act, and many implementations by Congress, put stringent regulations on the banking and mortgage industry. Predatory lending was the culprit.

To be a mortgage broker and/or an MLO or loan officer, one now needed to be licensed. The NMLS (National Mortgage Licensing Service) was established, and getting a license was no easy task. It required 20 hours of education, a national test and, for each individual state you wanted to be licensed in, a state test! Fees, a background check, a credit report, and fingerprints were also part of the process. I decided to get licensed. I signed up for the training course through Training Pro, Inc., one of the educational companies endorsed by the NMLS. They were great and I still use them today for continuing education. Everything is done online; the course, study materials, etc. I studied my ass off!

In the middle of 2009, I started to feel something like soap in my right eye. I ignored it! While going through this intense constant studying on the computer and with everything else happening, one day it hit me that I was having a problem seeing through my right eye. My left eye was perfect, and because of that it took me a long time to realize what was going on because I could see. One evening while at the ShopRite across from where I lived, I decided to stop into one of these retail eye care/eyewear stores. I told the gentleman what was going on, and he told me to come by the next morning to see the optometrist. The doctor took me in the back of the store where all of the equipment was, sat me down in front of this machine, and put me through some tests. My left eye was perfect in every way, but my right eye was another story. I was basically blind! I had glaucoma and my intraocular pressure was way up there! She wanted me to go to an ophthalmologist right away. I don't have time! I've got to play at Sunrise at 3:00 PM and I've got to be at PEOPLE at 6:00 PM! Plus, I've got to finish studying for a test scheduled for the following week! "My left eye is perfect; I'll live with it and deal with it later!"

A week later I took the NMLS National test. I scheduled it through a company called Pearson VUE; that was a mistake! Rude, unaccommodating people who didn't bathe often! A passing grade is 75: I got a 74. I failed! This may sound like sour grapes and maybe it is. The test was scheduled for 1:00 PM on May 10th. I got there and had to wait a half-hour after a check-in. They gave me a calculator that wasn't sufficient for a gnat, the smallest calculator they could find. There were calculations that had to be done. They gave me a scratch board with a scratch pen. In the middle of the test when it was time to calculate, the pen didn't write! I went to the proctor. Not only was she ugly, but she smelled! She gave me another pen; guess what: it didn't write, either! Obviously frustrated, I became a little testy. "Don't you check these things before you hand them out? (YOU

FUCKING MORON)!" Of course, I didn't say the last part! Bottom line, there are four parts to the test. I got a 90 on one part and in the 80s on two others. I got a 55 on the section that included the calculations and failed the entire test by ONE point. The law requires a 30-day wait before a retest.

I took the retest on June 20th. Changed the test center venue to Prometric. Nice, very professional people. Got there on time. Check-in was 10 minutes, the calculator was as big as a Kindle, and the pen was like a Sharpie! I got an 85! I took the New York test about 45 days later at the same place and got a 90! The test is just the beginning. After everything I previously mentioned, and because there was one blemish I was unaware of on my credit report, due to the bureaucracy at the New York State Department of Financial Services, I didn't get my license until February 2013!

Suffolk County

One Wednesday afternoon in April when I returned home from playing at Sunrise, I opened the door and found a business card on the floor that had been slipped through the mail slot. It was from Officer Vigilante at the Suffolk County Probation Department. On the reverse side was a handwritten note, "Please report Thursday, April 19th between 12:00 and 9:00 PM." I could tell it was from a woman by the handwriting.

I called her. "Suffolk County Probation Officer Vigilante," the young sweet voice answered. "Hi, it's Mr. Palermo!" "Michael," she replied! It was the last time she called me Michael! I went on to explain that I was out doing my community service and that I must have just missed her. She asked me if I was retired. When I informed her in a rather terse tone that I was a hard-working man paying tuition for two daughters, she replied in a terse tone of her own: "One thing I've learned is never to assume anything!" She seemed a little pissed off. After we hung up, I called her back and kind of apologized telling her I didn't want to get off on the wrong foot. She told me not to worry about it; she'd see me next Thursday.

I arrived at 11:50. The office of probation was in Edgewood. I had no idea where that was, so I MapQuested it and realized that it was by the Heartland Golf Park par 3 golf course on the border of Commack and Deer Park. I got there and, unlike Nassau, there was NO security guard, NO security walk through, just a sign-in sheet for each probation officer! I actually wondered why there was no security to protect the probation officers; any wacko could walk in there and who knows what could happen.

The place was rather dingy and the probationers were of a lower class. Naturally, I felt out of place dressed up in grey slacks, a blue polo shirt, and a sport coat. After about 15 minutes, the door opened and out walked this pretty little Italian gal with jet-black hair, green khaki jeans, and a grey pullover short-sleeved shirt. She picked up the clipboard with the sign in-sheet. "Michael Palermo." I stood up and we looked each other in the eye; we were kind of surprised. I think she was expecting a bald, fat, out-of-shape old man! I was expecting something similar in a woman! She walked me to a room in the back. There was a computer on her desk, and she immediately began typing as she asked me a few questions. I had to report to her every two months and had to call in if I were leaving the state or if there were any changes in my status. She kept me for about 15 minutes. I was smitten!

I reported to her two months later and every two months until she moved me to the next level in April 2013. Each visit was very professional—she called me Mr. Palermo! We chatted about being Italian, my daughters, how I was doing, and things in general. One day I got up the nerve to ask her what her first name was! She looked at me kind of funny and said, "Donna." Donna Vigilante! Nice!

Through conversation I found out her birthday was July 2nd. She was a Cancer! Typical Cancer, hard on the outside, soft on the inside. I've spent my life around them! Jenise, Nancy, the girl I lived with in Los Angeles, my ex-wife Rose, and my daughter Gina all are Cancer women! I really liked her; I found out she was 41 years old! Never had the balls to ask her if she was married, single, divorced, or whatever. I wanted to ask her out—how the hell do you ask your probation officer out? There is a line that I felt couldn't be crossed! I never did! Until this day I've thought about it.

In April 2013 I was moved to the next level of probation—I got promoted. Officer Vigilante had come to my place in late March; it was one of the requirements before I could be moved. She was supposed to move me a few months earlier but never did; maybe she didn't want to lose me. She was extremely fair with me, treated me with respect, and made my life easy. I believe she trusted me!

She showed up one Saturday afternoon about 2:30 PM with another officer I knew. He was my instructor in the Drinking Driver Program I had been through. His name was Mike. Coincidence? Maybe! He was Officer Vigilante's partner. They came upstairs, we chatted for a few minutes, and then Mike told me I had to blow. No problem! Naturally I blew a zero. I showed Officer Vigilante pictures of my daughters. She told me that she was moving me to the next level and I would have a new probation officer. "Can I call you Donna now?" "NOOOO!" We both laughed!

20

The Drinking Driver Program

Another mandatory portion of probation is the Drinking Driver Program, a seven-week course about the dangers and consequences of drinking and driving. I took it every Saturday morning from the second week in April 2012 right through Memorial Day Weekend, 10:00 AM to noon at South Oaks. There were about 15 people in the class and the instructor was Mike, the same Mike who showed up at my place with Officer Vigilante. We were given a workbook, there were lectures, there were videos, and there was discussion. The program dealt with prevention, reflection, and protection.

It was a relatively relaxed and painless experience. Mike was cool, a sports fan, most specifically a basketball fan. A Knicks fan! After class he and I would chat and I found out a little bit about him. He was from upstate New York and had relocated to Long Island about 20 years earlier. I gathered he was a police officer of some sort. When he showed up at my place, it confirmed my suspicions.

The Drinking Driver Program had limited rules: show up on time, don't miss a class or you'd have to start the entire program over, of course no drinking, do the work, and don't break Mike's balls. As I said it was painless! The only problem, again, was South Oaks. The sunshine and springtime weather made it a little better; but as I mentioned earlier, the place is depressing. It could use a facelift or at least a fresh coat of paint!

The Victim Impact Panel

For some reason, I think the thing that had the most profound effect on me was the Victim Impact Panel sponsored by MADD, Mothers Against Drunk Driving. Also mandatory, at this meeting there was a panel of people whose lives had been changed or altered by a DWI! I attended on Wednesday night, September 5, 2012. I had finished my 50 hours of community service at the end of June and I was pushing Will at PEOPLE to give me an early OASAS discharge. Will was steadfast in his strict belief that I would finish when he said I was finished. I liked him so I didn't fight him too much. I was discharged one week early and I think Will and the director, Bryant Kaplan, got together and decided that one week wasn't going to make a difference with me either way.

I was excited! It was the end of July and I was done with community service, I'd finished the Drinking Driver Program, and now I was finished with OASAS! MAYBE THEY'LL LET ME OFF EARLY! Not so fast. Everything had been sent over to Officer Vigilante. One day in the middle of August I had a voice message on my cell from Officer Vigilante; she wanted me to call her. "Maybe this is it! Maybe they're going to let me off and I can get this fucking thing out of my car!" The "thing" being the ignition interlock, which, I must confess, may be the WORST PART OF PROBATION!

I called her. She told me that she had received all of my information and there was another thing I had to go through! NO DISCHARGE, NO RELEASE FROM PROBATION, NO TAKING THE INTERLOCK OUT! There was disappointment in my voice and I said something stupid like "You didn't tell me!" She replied matter-of-factly: "Mr. Palermo, you seem to feel that you deserve some form of entitlement because you've finished these things early!" She was right and I was wrong—I told her that!

I asked her about the date of the panel. It was originally scheduled for Tuesday, September 4th. Between our conversation and the date of the panel I was scheduled for a probation meeting. Got there early as usual. She came out right at 12 noon! I noticed, for the first time since I met her, she had lipstick and a little eye makeup on. Adorable! She walked me back to the office and all of a sudden got apologetic with me. "The Impact Panel date has been changed from Tuesday the 4th to Wednesday the 5th. When they told me I thought of you . . . I hope it's not a problem!" I kind of laughed to myself because the 5th was opening night for the NFL and the Giants were playing Dallas! What could I say? No problem!

I showed up at 5:00 PM on the 5th. The meeting was held at the Suffolk County Office Building in Smithtown. There were about 100 people waiting outside for the doors to open. As I stood there and listened to the conversations taking place, something hit me. Most of these people were in denial! They had stories about why their particular DWI wasn't their fault! It was the cop, it was their wife's fault, they weren't really drunk, the breathalyzer was fixed, it was their sister's fault, it was their son's fault, they were right around the block from where they lived—

it was the fucking dog's fault, for chrissakes! I thought to myself: "AM I IN DENIAL?" And you know what? To some extent, I was! Not a severe denial but, nevertheless, some form of denial. From the beginning I wanted to place the blame and, throughout this book, I've tried to give an accurate account of how I actually felt at the particular moment I was writing about. I don't know why but right there, at that moment, it hit me! I DESERVED EVERYTHING I GOT!

Then I asked myself, "Why am I really so anxious to get probation over with?" Was it just the interlock or did I want a drink? As I was contemplating, the doors opened and we were told to come in. First there was a breathalyzer for each of us and then we went into an auditorium. An introductory speaker walked to the front. She gave us an overview of why the program was started, how it was put into place, what MADD was all about, and then introduced the first of three speakers. The first speaker was the wife of someone who had been killed by a drunk driver. She went through how she was informed about the incident, how it affected the lives of those in their family, and she told us a little about the man's life. Coincidentally, he was a high school and college wrestler and a few years older than me. I found it interesting that he too had wrestled at Nassau Community College.

The second speaker told about an incident that killed another member of her family. The third and most dramatic was a woman who lost her son. She relived the entire episode from saying goodbye to him as he was on his way to a school function, hearing sirens about a half-hour later, finding out that there had been an accident a few miles away but out of the area where her son could have possibly gone, then having the police come to her home and, ultimately, realizing that her son hadn't gone to the school at all! I found the entire evening powerful! On the way home, I once again began questioning myself. I realized that I did deserve to go through all of this, how lucky I was that I hadn't hurt or killed someone, and that the LAW is correct. Don't drink and drive! I once again asked myself why I wanted to get off probation. I resigned myself to the fact that it is what it is, and I'm just going to go through it for as long as it lasts, deal with it, and stop feeling sorry for myself!

22

Moving Right Along

After the Victim Impact Panel, I decided to just go with the flow. At the end of July I was informed by Bernie Hoyt, one of my former baseball players at St. Joseph's College, that our 1994 NAIA District 31 Championship team was going to be inducted into the St. Joseph's College Athletic Hall of Fame. It made me happy, not so much for myself but for the players on the team. It was a great team that performed during a special but controversial season. The controversy began before the season started and had nothing to do with the baseball program; it was all about the basketball program! The basketball coach, Joe Maniaci, and I were hired at the same time a year earlier. Joe was a good guy and, from all I could gather, a fine basketball coach. Fortunately for me, I inherited a program that had some talent. The previous coach had done a good job recruiting and building the program. I added the ingredients needed to put it over the top.

The basketball program was a mess! Very little talent and the NAIA District 31 was a strong conference in all sports. Joe had gotten his ass kicked the year before and was probably going to get his ass kicked again! In my opinion, he was worn out already;

and I don't believe he was as diligent in his recruiting efforts as he could have been. He wanted out of the NAIA; he wanted to move to a Division III schedule in the NCAA! He would have gotten his ass kicked there, too!

I had been in a similar situation when I became the head baseball coach at Suffolk Community College West in 1988. Basically there were no players, maybe 11 or 12 my first year. The conference we played in, Region XV in the NJCAA, was powerful and I got my ass kicked; but the day after the season I started to recruit and recruit. I went to every local high school, talked to each head coach, and spoke to each player individually. We made the playoffs my second, third, and fourth years and had three consecutive winning seasons. Then I got hired by St. Joe's.

I could be wrong, but I don't think Coach Maniaci was willing to recruit. He got into a big confrontation with Athletic Director, Frank Mulzoff. Frank was a stubborn SOB, but I liked him. He was a great basketball coach in his own right and a former head basketball coach at St. John's University. He took over at St. John's when Lou Carnesecca became the head coach of the New York Nets. Frank was at St. John's from 1971-1973, was the 1972 NCAA coach of the year, had a .675 winning percentage, and got fired. Why? Carnesecca couldn't coach in the pros, wanted to come back to St. John's, was a favorite son, and the AD at St. John's hated Frank. Frank was tough, brash, wasn't an ass kisser, liked to drink and, like I said, could be a son of a bitch. Similarly, for all of the same reasons, even though he had been there for 14 years, had started and built the athletic program from the ground up and did a magnificent job, I think the president of St. Joseph's, Sister Elizabeth Hill, wanted to get rid of him. So when Maniaci got through to the sister, she had the excuse she needed. I stuck up for Frank and was loyal to him. Though she liked me at the beginning of my tenure, because of my loyalty to Frank and because maybe I was a little like him, Sister Elizabeth became bitter toward me. I won the district, was the District 31 and CACC coach of the year, but had a tough season. Frank was fired just before the baseball season and I had no buffer between myself and the administration. Sister Elizabeth didn't help! In fact, she made my life miserable during and after the season ended. We had a bitter divorce! The years somewhat healed the wounds. The great 1994 baseball team got inducted into the Hall of Fame Friday, October 5, 2012; and I accepted the honor on their behalf. It turned out to be a great night. My daughters ,Mary and Gina, attended, I saw my former players, Frank was there, and I made what they tell me was a great acceptance speech!

The next big event in 2012 was Hurricane Sandy! Toward the end of October the National Weather Service began issuing severe wind and storm warnings for the tri-state area and Long Island specifically. Then the warnings turned into hurricane warnings. They were right! Long Island got nailed big time. Houses were destroyed, roads were wiped out, telephone and electric poles were ripped out of the ground, cars were smashed, people were injured, and some lost their lives.

The South Shore of Long Island was devastated both in Nassau and Suffolk counties. The garage at my house in Bethpage where my daughters were staying was destroyed. My neighbors' tree was uprooted and took out two of the trees on my property and smashed the roof. The roof in the back of the house was also partially damaged. Thank God no one was hurt. Because my in-laws had lost all of the electricity in their house, they stayed at that house with my ex-wife. To accommodate them, my daughter Gina spent a little over a week with me! It was a pleasure to have her.

After the storm subsided, one Sunday morning I took a ride down to the beach on the shore of the Great South Bay in Babylon. The devastation that took place was clear. One particular house that stood on the curve of the road that approached the beach looked like Godzilla had stepped on the roof and squashed and flattened it into a pile of debris. The dock and the pier at Bergen Point that had been rebuilt after the previous hurricane were completely ripped out! So in two years, 2011 and 2012, we had two hurricanes. The one in 2011 was minor league. Sandy won the World Series!

The end of the year and the holiday season were relatively uneventful. I spent Thanksgiving alone. The girls came over for breakfast, I went to church, and I spent the rest of the day writing, playing the guitar, and watching football. The Jets were playing the Patriots in a hyped-up night game. The Jets got destroyed and the quarterback, Mark Sanchez, became involved in one of the funniest plays of all time: The Butt Fumble. If you don't know what it is or never saw it, "Google" it. Words can't describe it.

I spent Christmas Eve with my daughters, Christmas Day with my cousins, and New Year's Eve at a party at the home of my friend, Joe Chetti. For the first time in I don't know how long, I spent the entire holiday season sober—not a drop!!!

23

2013

New Year's Day 2013 was spent in relative obscurity. Quiet and restful! Mary and Gina came over for breakfast; and after they left, I took a ride down to the beach. I wanted to see how the cleanup was progressing since my last visit. The house on the curve was still a pile, the roads were still damaged, the dock was still gone, but the cleanup was under way. I stopped in church for a little while, came home and watched a little football and decided about 4:00 PM that I was going for Chinese food. I had a desire. I have to desire Chinese food; it's not something I think about often. So I went to a place off Montauk Highway in Lindenhurst. I had miso soup, a spring roll and vegetable chop suey, tea as my beverage—with a dish of chocolate ice cream and a fortune cookie! I went home and decided against a cigar—I felt somewhat cleansed by the vegetarian meal! Put the robe and slippers on and I was in bed and asleep by 9:00 PM.

In the middle of January my buddy Scott had to go in the hospital for what basically amounted to an operation to remove a blockage in an artery in his lower back. He had been complaining about lower back pain for a few years. Scott, the lawyer I referred to earlier in the book, was a chain smoker. He smoked at least two packs of cigarettes a day, maybe more. I met him through his father, Myron Brenker. Myron, or Mike as he called himself, was someone I had known since 1973 when I worked as a major appliance salesman for Sears. I was a kid and Mike was 20 years my senior. We hit it off and through him, a few years after I moved back from Los Angeles, Scott, nine years younger than me, and I became friends, very good friends, almost a brother-like relationship.

Mike, also an extremely heavy smoker, passed away due to complications from emphysema in 2010! I kept telling Scott to stop smoking; his body would cleanse and maybe his arteries would open up. He also slept on a couch in a very awkward position that lent itself to just the kind of pain he was experiencing. He wouldn't listen and he was living through a series of very depressing events. Not only did he lose a father who he was close to but also his wife, a girl he had imported from China. She had deserted him for the homeland.

Scott wanted the American dream! A house in the suburbs, a wife, a child, and a black lab! He had the house, has yet to attain the wife and child, but he bought the black lab. He got her in May of 2012 as a surprise for his wife when she returned from her visit to China. The wife never returned, but he had the dog —her name is Missy.

Scott went in for surgery, caught C-diff, and what was supposed to be a four-day stay at NYU Medical Center turned into five weeks. They almost killed him. When I went to see him in the hospital, he was a mess. He wasn't the only mess. NYU was disgusting, filthy dirty and they were sandblasting the halls. No wonder he got a virus!

When he returned home, he was very weak. His mother was staying with him and taking care of him. Missy had been in a kennel for five weeks and was as hyper as she could be. She was too much for Scott's mother. He asked me take care of Missy. I am a dog lover. The Sunday I visited Scott at home, I gave him a shave and I took Missy for a long walk. Missy and I bonded. When I returned from the walk, he asked me again. I wanted her, but I had a one bedroom co-op on the second floor and no backyard. I explained this to him. I told him to give it a few more days.

A couple of days later he called me pleading. The dog was driving his mother, and consequently him, insane! I agreed to take her for a few days until he got stronger. A few days turned into two weeks. I loved having her, but it wasn't a good situation. A great dog, she reminded me so much of Charlie the black lab/Airedale mix I bought for my children. Charlie lived for 14 years. He was the best. I loved him. He was my buddy and loved the family. He got sick from old age, and I had to put him down in 2007. I cried for three days. Anyway, I'd walk Missy twice a day, train her, take her to the park and run her; but it wasn't enough. She needed a house with a yard. At the beginning of the third week this became apparent. I wasn't home enough! Though she never had an accident on my new carpet, she'd eat my gloves and papers on my desk, dig holes in the walls, tear up toys, etc. I had to find her a good home. Scott wasn't capable of taking her back! I began making phone calls to everyone I knew and finally hit the jackpot with Joe Chetti. Although they had three already, he and his wife were dog lovers and were looking for another. I brought her over to the house on a Saturday morning and left her. I never saw her again. It broke my heart!

24

End Game

In March 2013 I met my new probation officer, Gary Diamond. I reported to him, submitted to a urine test, and discussed my case. He told me the next time I had to report was July 5th. I was to call in every month on the 25th, the day I was born in May. We had a nice chat and I found him to be very cordial. I continued on with my probation—working, singing, playing the guitar, but no drinking.

One Saturday morning at the end of February, I walked into a coffee shop, All the Perks, in the ShopRite center across from where I lived. I noticed the place when it first opened in September 2012. A singer/guitar player was performing. I grabbed a cup of coffee, sat down, and listened. After finishing I asked the girl at the counter if there were any openings for performers. She told me to come back Monday morning and speak to the owner/manager, Maureen. Maureen told me that there was an opening from noon to 2:00 PM on Saturdays. I could come in the following Saturday and if she liked me, she'd keep me. She liked me!

I played there every Saturday using my stage name Erik Kyle. It paid 5 bucks an hour plus tips. I didn't care—just enjoyed playing and it kept me occupied. The tips turned out to be pretty good. I'd average between 10 and 15 bucks. One Saturday I walked out of there with close to 30 bucks in tips plus the 10 bucks in pay—in two hours I made 40 bucks! Great! So every Saturday I'd get up, go to the gym for a workout, shower, go to DD for coffee, come home, check my email, and go play.

On my birthday, Saturday, May 25th, my daughters took me to B.B. King's in New York City to see the Beatles tribute band, Strawberry Fields. I took the train in and met them there. While waiting for the train, I made my call to probation. Officer Diamond's voicemail answered and, as I did in April, I left my standard call-in message. The show at B.B. King's was great! I walked into the club and downstairs, where a full brunch was waiting with a cash bar. I drank coffee with my eggs, bacon, sausage, French toast, home fries, brownies, and apple pie. The band was terrific. The first hour, dressed in early Beatle suits and Beatle wigs, they played all of the Beatles' early music, from "She Loves You" to "Eight Days a Week" to "Help." After a 10-minute intermission, they came out in full Sergeant Pepper garb and played songs from the balance of the Beatle Era, the "psychedelic" through the "*Abbey Road*" and "*Let It Be*" albums. We had a wonderful time!

One Sunday morning in early June I got a call from Brian, the guy who installed my Interceptor ignition interlock device. He told me that Interceptor completely lost its contract with the state and that I might have to change my interlock company. He told me that some people who were near the end of their probation were allowed to lose the thing completely. No such luck for me! The following Tuesday I got a call from Officer Diamond and he explained the situation to me. I had to call Intoxalock, set up a new account, and replace the device at no charge! Great! Just when I was used to that girl telling me to "PLEASE WAIT!"

Brian picked up the contract with Intoxalock, and he would be able to make the switch. So I made an appointment and got it done. The new device didn't speak; it TWEETED! Although much bigger and more cumbersome than the Interceptor, it did have a few advantages. It had a digital timer that showed a countdown in seconds. After you shut off the engine of the car, there were two minutes allotted where you were able to restart the vehicle without having to blow. It was the same on the Interceptor device but without the digital timer, so you had to guess! The camera was also placed in a different location, on the windshield by the passenger side and was much smaller and less noticeable. Again, I was resigned and did what I had to do.

On July first Gina turned 23 years old. I couldn't believe that my little girl, my GG, reached that plateau. She'd grown up to be a beautiful lady. Much of that credit goes to her mother! Though we had our differences, I always knew that Rose had our children's best interests at heart. One of the caveats in our divorce agreement was that when Gina turned 23 we would sell the house and split the profits. My lease was up where I lived, so I decided to buy her out. I wanted to move back to a house and had been looking for one when I got into DWI trouble. We came to an agreement, and I was to move back to 21 Ginny Lane in Bethpage on September 1.

I went to see Officer Diamond and explained the situation. It didn't seem to faze him. "You're not moving to Florida, so I'll worry about it when I have to!" We had a nice meeting, discussed the par 3 golf course near the probation center and the new interlock device. When he asked me how I liked it, he told me if it was up to him I wouldn't have it too much longer. He set our next meeting for October 10th. I left him that day hoping he was telling me that the end was near, but I wasn't counting on it.

I began moving the last week in August. Rose left the place immaculate so there was little for me to do. On Saturday, August 31, I was completely moved in. Monday, September 2 was Labor Day. On Tuesday morning September 3rd, 18 months to the day I began probation, at about 10:30 AM, as I was driving, my cell phone rang. It was Officer Diamond! "Mr. Palermo . . . " I'll leave the rest to your imagination. MY PROBATION WAS OVER! Officer Diamond gave me specific instructions. I was to come to the office, pick up my release papers, take one to the DMV first and get my license restriction for the interlock removed and then, and only then, take the car to Brian and get the thing taken out. I couldn't thank Officer Diamond enough.

No one is perfect. We all make mistakes. Hopefully we learn from those mistakes and try not to make the same mistake twice. Did I have too much to drink that night? Yes! Did I deserve everything I went through? Absolutely! Did I learn my lesson? I hope so! Is there any message in all of this? I don't know! But I'll tell you something: I'm a child of the '60s. I grew up with marijuana: I smoked it, inhaled it, sucked it down to the roach, and then ate the roach. Then there was cocaine! I did that, too! Never liked it but almost became addicted to it. Athletics, especially playing tennis every day, made me stop!

There was always alcohol! Beer, wine, vodka, scotch, bourdon, whiskey, anisette, cognac, etc.! Why and how does one become an abuser? A great question! Does therapy help? Another great question! I think that all the therapy in the world, all the professional discussions in the world, only help if there is self-help—if there is the desire inside!

"It seems to me we're better off consulting with our souls," a wise man said! Being completely sober for 18 months made me realize how wonderful and refreshing it is to be clean! Will I ever drink again? Probably, but responsibly! I promised myself I would NEVER drink and drive again! The next time I think about drinking and driving I'm going to read this book! Bottom line—DON'T DRINK and DRIVE! The next time you think about it, maybe you should read this book!

Afterword

I have been a Police Officer for nearly 16 years. After graduating from the Academy I was assigned to day shifts for four months and then switched to night shifts, which I did not mind because I'm a night owl. I quickly became involved in the world of DWIs (Driving While Intoxicated.)

At first I would assist other seasoned Officers on their traffic stops. I would watch and learn how to interact with intoxicated drivers. Car stops in general are considered to be one of the most dangerous interactions with the public. One has no idea who he or she is stopping. An Officer stops a vehicle for a simple Vehicle and Traffic Law (VTL) infraction and, unbeknownst to the Officer, the occupant or occupants of the vehicle might be having much bigger problems than just a defective tail light. After the initial contact with the operator, an Officer might become suspicious that the driver is intoxicated. In order to further investigate, the Officer should ask the operator to step out of the vehicle. This is where it gets difficult. Nobody likes to get stopped by the Police! Nobody likes to be told what to do!

One has to master the skills of an expert negotiator combined with a psychologist. Not wanting to be overbearing, at the same time the Officer has to be the one who controls the scene. I don't want to get into all the different scenarios, but one can only imagine how complex it could be to deal with an intoxicated individual.

After months and months of riding the coattails of the senior Officers, I finally started to make my own arrests. Many of them. Not everyone who sings knows how to sing and only a few make it to stardom. I became an opera singer.

I believe that I became quite experienced in the world of the DWI. With that being said, unfortunately I also became jaded. Why? Because not everyone I ever stopped who was under the influence, did I arrest. There were many situations where I gave people a second chance.

I am not God. I don't think that I am always right, but I try to be as understanding as I could be. So I get it. We all make mistakes. Unfortunately the truth is that the vast majority of people who get arrested for DWI have been driving drunk for many many times before they get arrested. It's a fact. The first time someone gets drunk, he or she is usually too scared to drive. As time goes on and they see that nothing happened, people become more complacent. Or brave? Hence the saying: "Beer muscle."

Alcohol is a funny substance. It helps people to get rid of their inhibitions, and lack of judgment sets in. Therefore it is extremely difficult to argue with intoxicated persons. Most of the time they are convinced that they are right and they are fine. I have asked people to leave their car parked and get a ride. Or I have given them a ride home myself. Just to see them later, returning to their cars and driving them away themselves.

I have arrested the same people multiple times for the same DWI offense. We all have this belief in us that says: "It can't happen to me."

It's an absolute tragedy what happens on the road. People's lives get ruined in a matter of seconds. Many fun-filled nights end in horror - body parts all over the road, people crying and telling me that "he (or she) looked fine." They themselves are drunk, so they can't judge themselves, much less their friend or relative who drove. Few people are able to take responsibility for their actions. We live in a society where everything is someone else's fault. Perfect examples are those parked cars damaged over the weekend. These drunken acts usually happen after 4 in the morning, and nobody takes responsibility for them.

I was very upset to get that call from Mr. Palermo. I knew exactly what the legal ramifications could be. Getting arrested is not fun. Especially for someone who never had any run-ins with the law. It feels humiliating. To deal with it emotionally could be a challenge. And losing your privilege to operate a motor vehicle is a huge thing. Especially if one lives in such a region as Long Island, where mass transportation is an absolute disaster.

Given my personal experience regarding how people don't learn their lesson, I was also worried that this first arrest was just going to be the beginning of a downhill spiral for Mr. Palermo.

He proved me wrong. Thank God.

I am so happy to see that he was able to overcome this difficult obstacle. He is one of the few. I wish to have more people like him out there. Hopefully his book will help people to overcome their own problems, or maybe prevent them from becoming a problem themselves.

P.S. To get people to submit to a preliminary breath test (PBT) could be difficult. In most cases those people who refuse it have been arrested before for the same, or they listened to too many stories from their friends or lawyers.

The truth is that if one is an experienced Officer and a keen observer, then even without a PBT he could come to an appropriate conclusion. I have proved to many people that taking the PBT is not a guarantee one will get arrested. As a matter of fact, it could actually help. Some people act extremely strangely even after consuming a very little amount of alcohol. By providing a sample, one could prove that he or she really didn't drink a lot.

One beer, one shot, one 8-ounce glass of wine all contain the same amount of alcohol - .02% generally. A healthy body metabolizes .02% per hour. So technically one could drink one beer every hour and never get to .08%, which is the legal limit. Everyone always said: "I had 2 drinks" and they blow at .14% or more.

So, what did they really drink? They either lie, or they are legitimately too drunk to judge themselves. All lawyers will always tell people not to provide a sample. I have proven that to be wrong advice, not just once, but many times. But this would be an endless debate.

~ Z

About the Author

Michael Anthony Palermo was born May 25, 1950 in Brooklyn, New York to his parents Violet (Adamo) and Pasquale Palermo. In 1959 the family moved to Levittown, New York. He graduated from Island Trees High School in Levittown where he was on the Varsity Wrestling and Baseball Teams. He graduated from Hofstra University in 1972 with a Bachelor's Degree in Business. While in college he also wrestled and played baseball. In addition, he plays the guitar and began writing songs, poetry and journalistic essays at an early age.

In 1974 he relocated to Los Angeles, California to pursue a career in entertainment. After spending ten years on the West

Coast, he moved back to Long Island, New York in 1984 where he met his wife Rosemarie. They have three beautiful daughters. While living in Los Angeles he began coaching baseball and continued to do so on Long Island. In 1989 he was named the Heal Baseball Coach at Suffolk Community College in Brentwood, New York. In 1992 he was named the Head Baseball Coach at St. Joseph's College in Patchogue, New York where he led the Golden Eagles to the 1994 NAIA District 31 Baseball Championship. He was named the 1994 NAIA District 31 and the CACC Baseball Coach of the Year.

He currently resides on Long Island. He has been a successful Life and Health Insurance Broker and Mortgage Loan Officer for over 30 years.

www.ingramcontent.com/pod-product-compliance
Lightning Source LLC
Chambersburg PA
CBHW060616080526
44585CB00013B/853